Collins

creating garden
PONDS
and water features

creating garden
PONDS
and water features

DEBBIE ROBERTS AND IAN SMITH

First published in 2001 by
HarperCollins*Publishers*
77–85 Fulham Palace Road
Hammersmith
London W6 8JB

The HarperCollins website address is www.**fire**and**water**.com

Collins is a registered trademark of HarperCollins Publishers Limited

02 04 06 07 05 03 01
2 4 6 8 9 7 5 3 1

Produced by Kingfisher Design, London
Design & Project Director: Pedro Prá-Lopez
Designer: Frances Prá-Lopez
Editor: Diana Rayner
Index: Hilary Bird
Plant authenticator for Chapter 7, Plant Selector: Barbara Segall
Text for Chapter 8, Fish Selector: Steve Windsor, *Practical Fishkeeping*
Illustrations: Debbie Roberts and Ian Smith, Acres Wild

A catalogue record of this book is available from the British Library

ISBN 0 00 710660 2

Colour reproduction by Colourscan, Singapore
Printed and bound by Printing Express Ltd, Hong Kong

Contents

Introduction

Water is the key to life itself and is one of the most captivating elements that can be introduced into the garden; the interplay of water and light can dazzle the eye, lift the spirit and create a powerful added dimension to the whole garden experience. This book aims to identify the ways in which the qualities of water can be exploited in the garden and guides you through the process of creating a pond or water feature that is specific to your particular site and reflects your individual tastes and requirements.

We start by looking at sources of inspiration and some of the many ways that water can be introduced, while stressing the need to consider the context within which your pond or water feature is placed. It is important that it complements the character and style of the rest of your garden; the aim is to create an integrated composition with water as a key ingredient. This is true whether you are creating a completely new water garden or looking to refresh or update an existing one. To this end we have explored the thinking behind a number of successful water gardens and reworked them to show how a pond or water feature can be styled in a variety of ways to create different effects within a garden of a particular size and setting.

Once you have decided on the style and type of your pond or water feature and where it will be located in your garden, you will need to tackle its installation.

Chapter 5 leads you through the practical aspects of this, with step-by-step sequences showing how to create various types of feature and detailed information on pond liners and edgings to help you achieve a successful result. Creating a pond allows you to grow a whole new range of garden plants and Chapter 6 reveals how to choose and use plants to complement your pond and help integrate it into the rest of your garden.

One of the most satisfying aspects of water gardening is the contribution it can make to wildlife conservation. Designing ponds to attract wildlife is examined in some depth to help you create your own mini nature reserve. You may wish to enliven your pond further with ornamental fish, and their needs and requirements are discussed in a separate chapter, together with a range of suitable species from which to choose.

As with all aspects of gardening, the creation of your pond or water feature is only the beginning of the story. Gardens evolve and grow and the pond will also continue to develop and mature over time. Having spent time and effort on its creation it is important that you carefully manage the subsequent changes throughout the year and over time. To help with this we have outlined the necessary tasks in a seasonal maintenance table to keep your pond or water feature in top condition and give you pleasure for many years to come.

Top and left: **As garden designers we regard water as a powerful, expressive and essential ingredient. In this garden our intention was to make water the major theme and to use it in a variety of different ways, from a formal rill and reflecting pool close to the house to a large informal pond and waterfall at the bottom of the garden**

Debbie Roberts and Ian Smith

1 • Inspiration

Water exerts such enduring fascination that many people would put it close to the top of their wish list for inclusion in the garden. If you are considering bringing water into your garden, think first about what attracted you to the idea. Was it the qualities of water itself or a landscape or water garden that you have seen or visited? Sources of inspiration are important as they provide you with the enthusiasm to be creative and make something that is unique to you.

Clockwise from left: **The captivating effects of water reflecting architectural elements, colour and light, and willow trees**

Qualities of water

Water can be serene and calming, lively and refreshing or powerful and exhilarating. Perhaps its most striking quality is its ability to reflect light, creating mirror images in still pools and fragmented patterns where the surface is agitated. Water can also drip and bubble to create concentric ripples across the surface or it can foam and froth, creating air bubbles that turn the water white. Spurts of water can make playful or graceful dancing effects in the air. Flowing water provides a sense of movement, while falling and splashing water can create exciting visual effects with sounds to match.

Clockwise from top left: A graceful foaming geyser, gently bubbling fountains and ripples, playful water jets and an exhilarating cascade

Water gardens past and present

Water has played a central role in the gardens of many different cultures throughout the ages, used for its practical, aesthetic and symbolic qualities. Historical precedents can provide an excellent source of inspiration for your own water garden.

Oriental influences

Perhaps the most ancient tradition of water in garden design lies in China, where a complex mix of symbolism and Taoist philosophy had great influence. In gardens this expressed itself through an interpretation of the natural world, with its landscapes of mountain and water. The concept of using the natural elements of water and stone was developed still further in Japan, where the art of garden design was elevated to a high status. Gardens made in this tradition symbolize man's relationship with nature and are still highly influential around the world.

Islamic influences

A different tradition developed in arid regions of the world, where water was an essential element of the development of civilization. The technique of channelling water for

Clockwise from top left: A modern interpretation of Japanese garden design representing natural landscape; Islamic gardens of the Alhambra and the Generalife in Granada, begun about 1250

irrigation was paralleled by the development of water gardens that in time grew to become the Islamic Paradise Garden. Here the concept of Paradise, described in the Koran as a garden, was made real. In contrast to the oriental gardens, there was no attempt to make the garden appear natural; water was employed for its cooling properties in the form of fountains, basins, pools and rills within enclosed courtyards.

The Renaissance and beyond

A more spectacular and ornamental approach to water garden design developed during the Renaissance period in 15th- and 16th-century Italy. The garden became a place of pleasure where water was celebrated, with elaborate fountains and cascades adding excitement and vitality. This approach to garden design drew upon the classical past of Ancient Rome, but also looked ahead to the modern era. The use of water as a spectacular garden element continued throughout Europe in grand formal schemes, culminating in the gardens at Versailles in France and in the naturalistic landscape gardens of 18th-century England.

The modern era

It was not until the late 19th and early 20th century that garden design developed on a more intimate and domestic scale, linking the garden to the house. Water was still a key element but was used in a more restrained way with formal reflecting pools, small fountains and rills. The traditional Arts and Crafts approach, personified by the work of Edwin Lutyens and Gertrude Jekyll, still holds great influence over garden design

today. The contrasting approach of what can broadly be called Modernism created a more functional and uncluttered use of space, resulting in the garden being increasingly seen as an outside room.

Water plays an essential role in contemporary garden design, still drawing on historical influences, but now less dictated by tradition or culture and more concerned with individual style and personal taste.

Top to bottom: Spectacular fountains and cascades at the Villa D'Este at Tivoli, built in 1550; the traditional formality of the Lutyens/Jekyll garden at Hestercombe in Somerset, completed in 1908; and the minimalist modernity of the Mies Van Der Rohe Pavilion in Barcelona of 1929

Inspiration from home and abroad

Visiting gardens and observing the ways in which water is used can provide an endless source of ideas for your own garden. Although many gardens open to the public may be quite large and grand they will always contain elements that can be adapted. Visits to other countries can expose you to exciting gardens from different traditions, but inspiration can also come from your local landscape. Observing water in nature will give you clues as to how to treat it in the garden.

Clockwise from left: **The Majorelle garden, Marrakech; a courtyard in Barcelona; Wakehurst Place Gardens, Sussex**

Above: The stillness and tranquillity of natural ponds and the arrangement of plants in simple masses is a lesson from nature in good design

Left: International garden shows such as those at Hampton Court and Chelsea showcase many design ideas and are good places to see water used in innovative and contemporary ways

Right: Studying the way in which water moves to create natural waterfalls is essential in successfully creating such features in your own garden

2 • Design Choices

Having been inspired to bring water into your garden you can now consider the form that it will take, for example a still pool or a moving watercourse, a raised pond or a self-contained fountain. Whatever type of pond or water feature you create, it is important to choose a style that will reflect the character of the garden and the house to which it belongs. This might be formal, asymmetric or informal depending upon whether a traditional, contemporary or naturalistic look is appropriate for the particular location.

Left and below: **Formality is achieved here through regularly spaced blocks of clipped box containing avenue trees placed**

Formality

Formality is created by order and symmetry through regular compositions balanced about a central axis, often with focal points to draw the eye. The style is clear, controlled and classical and suits gardens adjoining grander or more traditional houses, although the use of modern materials will create a more contemporary interpretation (see show garden page 13). A formal pond will be geometric and regular in shape, either sunken or raised, with well-defined architectural edgings complemented by restrained planting.

between canals and in a still reflecting pool set symmetrically about a central axis. A garden bench is located on the cross axis

Asymmetry

Asymmetry is a design style created where the elements of the composition are balanced and ordered, but in a manner that is offset rather than symmetrical. It creates a more relaxed and contemporary feel, often achieved by overlapping or interconnecting shapes, making it more dynamic and exciting than a formal arrangement yet more obviously designed and controlled than a informal one. An asymmetric pond will be geometric or angular, albeit not necessarily regular, in shape. It can be sunken or raised, isolated or interconnected, and complemented by controlled or more naturalistic planting.

Below and below right: By offsetting the spillways in interconnecting raised ponds and setting regular stepping stones to one side of a formal sunken pond, an asymmetrical balance can be successfully achieved

Above: The components of this modernist design are balanced despite the lack of symmetry

Informality

Informality in the garden is achieved through designing softly flowing curves and shapes to create a very natural appearance. Edges are blurred and the transitions from one shape or area to another are gradual. An informal pond will have gently sloping sides and a soft outline disguised by plants or natural materials such as pebbles, as is the case with wildlife ponds and oriental-style water gardens. The inspiration comes from nature rather than an imposed idea of order, and the result is therefore sympathetic to more natural or rural situations or to the further reaches of a garden rather than an area close to the house. That is not to say that more formal elements cannot be incorporated, as often the contrast between man-made order and the apparent chaos of nature can create very pleasing compositions.

Above and below: Focal points such as plants with strong forms and contemporary sculpture are enhanced when they are viewed against an informal backdrop

Above and below: The informality of a flowing line of candelabra primulas (*Primula* sp.) is suggestive of a naturally occurring, informal stream. The informal appearance of this oriental water garden is in fact created through very considered design

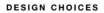

Clockwise from top: An informal pond can be given a more designed appearance by the inclusion of carefully composed ornamental planting and pebble beaches, whereas the natural effect of a wildlife pond is achieved through the intermingling of native plants

Sunken and raised ponds

An important decision you will need to take about your pond is whether the water surface will lie below the surrounding ground level or be raised above it. The choice you make will affect the character of your pond and will depend upon a number of factors, from child safety to the location of the pond within the garden.

Above: **This formal sunken pond has a slightly raised edge that has been decorated with ceramic tiles**

Below: **Adjacent to a seating area, this pond has been raised to seat level and fitted with a slatted top to allow closer access to the water**

Sunken ponds

In nature, water collects in low-lying areas, creating ponds whose size and shape is dictated by the contours of the ground. Sunken ponds with the water surface lying below the level of the surrounding ground appear to settle comfortably into the garden even where they have a deliberately formal appearance. They can be any size or

Above: **The circular shape of this sunken pond is reflected by the concentric ripples sent out by the central fountain**

Left: This raised pond, fed by a matching spillway, makes an ideal water feature adjacent to a wall or boundary. It has been faced with timber boards, stained to complement the glazed containers

Below and below left: A raised pond is safer for young children, especially when it is fitted with a protective grille. Although the primary purpose of a grille is practical there is no need for it to be unsightly, as this metal one with lily pad decoration shows

shape and edged with any material, hard or soft, and are the obvious choice for an informal and naturalistic feature or a wildlife pond. Brimming ponds are those where the water level is flush with the surrounding surface (see page 81).

Raised ponds

Raised ponds effectively lift up the surface of the water and allow you closer contact, particularly if you make the walls and rim wide enough to sit on. This makes them an ideal choice for elderly or disabled gardeners as well as potentially safer features for very young children who could easily fall into sunken ponds. Raised ponds suit formal or asymmetric designs and,

being built features, relate well to the architecture and hard landscape associated with terraces and patios close to the house. To achieve a successful result it is important to key a raised pond into the built landscape and construct it from matching materials. Raised ponds and water features require some practical skills for installation, but they reduce the amount of excavated soil to be removed and so may be an option where there is no obvious place in the garden for the excess soil.

Flowing and falling water

To provide your pond with a greater sense of movement and vitality, or to exploit a slope in your garden, you might consider a flowing water feature in the form of a stream or rill. Streams are intended as natural-looking features creating a sense of informality, whereas rills are clearly man-made features that are formal in character.

Only the slightest slope is needed to move water from one part of the garden to another, but a steeper level change allows you the opportunity to create more dramatic effects with waterfalls, chutes, cascades and staircases. Falling water creates an increased feeling of movement as well as a captivating sound that can counteract obtrusive sources of noise such as busy roads. It can also oxygenate the pond water to help keep it clear and healthy for fish and other pond life.

Clockwise from top: Water can flow gently along rills, fall dramatically over rocks or descend gracefully over water staircases

Clockwise from top left:
Flowing water can be
informal as in deep rocky
pools and shallow rippling
streams or formal as in the
rills below, one narrow and
shallow and the other wide
and deep

Sources

All moving or falling water in the garden will have a source and a destination. In an artificial system the destination is a pond or reservoir that receives all the water from where a pump returns it to the source. The outlet through which water begins its journey can be as natural or artificial as you wish, depending on the effect that you want to achieve. It can be hidden with rocks or plants to create the illusion of water issuing from a natural origin or it can become an eye-catching feature in its own right.

Clockwise from top left: A source can be traditional such as a classical mask, modern as in this perspex water chute, naturalistic, minimalist, prehistoric or even sexy!

Falls

Waterfalls are formed where a change in level occurs in streams and rills and between two or more interconnected ponds. Water can be made to project beyond the face of a fall, creating a smooth sheet, or to cling to the surface, producing a rippling cascade effect. It can be speeded up by channelling it through narrow spillways or slowed down by allowing it to fall across wider openings. Whatever the style of the pond or watercourse, the design of a fall or spill should always enhance its appearance.

Clockwise from left: Here a series of naturalistic waterfalls and modernist cascades show multi-tiered falling water, while an informal fall and a contemporary spillway are examples of single-tier designs

Crossing water

Water has a strongly magnetic appeal and where access over the surface is possible the attraction is even greater. Crossing your pond or stream allows you a completely different view of the water and adds to your enjoyment of the feature. However, it is important that any crossing is part of a route round or through the garden and placed at a seemingly natural point, often where the stretch of water is at its narrowest.

Stepping stones

Stepping stones are a particularly inviting way to cross water and less imposing than a bridge. They lead the eye across and can impart a feeling of fun and excitement. Regular stones set in a straight line suggest order and formality in an architectural setting, while circular or natural stones following a meandering line are relaxed in feel and suit a more informal setting. Choosing materials or shapes that appear elsewhere in the garden will integrate the stepping stones into the wider garden composition.

Above: **A crossing over water is always irresistible**

Clockwise from right: **Irregular stepping stones suit informal ponds while circular stones, cast from steel or concrete, mimic ripples in a contemporary pond and lily pads in a naturalistic setting**

Bridges

Bridges have a more permanent and imposing feel than stepping stones and can form a real focal point in the garden, so it is vital that you choose both the style and positioning of the bridge carefully. It is particularly important that bridges are placed to form part of a route, as a bridge that leads nowhere will look contrived and false and may actually detract from the appearance of your pond or stream.

Many styles and types of bridge are possible, from simple spans of timber or stone to more grand and elaborate designs. To ensure success, use materials that match or combine well with those used for your pond or elsewhere in the garden.

Below, left to right: **Simple bridges across narrow streams can be made from old railway sleepers or single pieces of rough or cut stone**

Above: **Here a Monet-style bridge is reflected in a waterlily pond**

Above: A traditional fountain is centrally located within this formal raised pond

Below: A ceramic spill pan is mounted on the side of this contemporary raised pond

Fountains and features

Fountains introduce energy and vitality to the garden pond, bringing the elements of air and water together as water is forced upwards in order to fall back down again. Because sunshine reflects from the droplets of water, fountains seem to capture light, especially when viewed against a dark background. As the water falls it cools and refreshes the air through which it moves, creating pleasant sounds as it strikes the water surface below. Gently bubbling or spilling fountains will create a sense of calm, while more vigorous fountains and curtains will

Above: Here a drilled boulder fountain creates a sculptural centrepiece in an informal pond

Left: A shimmering water curtain creates a transparent barrier between one part of the garden and another

generate feelings of excitement with their splashing.

A wide range of fountainheads and outlets are available to create various effects and features from simple jets and sprays to foaming boulders, brimming bowls and more sophisticated sculptural pieces. A fountain will always draw your attention, so it is important to locate it carefully and choose a feature that will suit the style of your garden. Fountains can either be set into the pond itself or mounted to the side to spill into the water. They can even be suspended above, as in the case of a water curtain, where water is pumped up to an overhead pipe or rail that is perforated to allow it to spill back down through the holes. Fountains can also be installed without the need for a pond (see page 28).

Right: A pergola structure fitted with chains allows water to trickle down into the pond below

Above: **This thread-like fountain journeys through the air in intermittent pulses**

Above: **A revolving copper fountainhead adds vitality to the garden pond by spinning water off in all directions**

Reservoir fountains

Even if you have no space for a pond you can still enjoy the sounds and effects of a fountain as it can just as easily be fed with water from a concealed reservoir. Reservoir fountain features with no open water are ideal where child safety is a concern. They can be either stood on a surface or mounted on a wall, although if the water falls into a container or trough before returning to the concealed reservoir you must make sure that children cannot fall or climb into the water.

The choice of fountainhead and outlet is extremely wide, the most popular types being drilled boulders and brimming urns for freestanding features and wall masks and spouts with associated containers or troughs for wall-mounted fountains. If you want to create something unique there is no reason why you should not adapt other containers or found objects for the purpose or even commission a piece of sculpture.

Again, locating your fountain with care is crucial to its success as it will always be a focal point in the garden. You might place it near a favourite seat where you will be spending time or

Above: **Here a steel hemisphere fountain draws the eye in a contemporary garden; glass beads hide the reservoir**

perhaps choose the middle of a planted bed or the end of a vista where it can be enjoyed from a variety of places within the garden. The important thing is to integrate it into its setting so that it will not appear disconnected and isolated.

Below: **A drilled stone fountain is a focal point in an informal garden; the reservoir is concealed beneath creeping plants**

Above: Fountain features need to be placed carefully in the garden. This figurative piece by Desmond Fountain is placed beneath a weeping pear tree and surrounded with plants and pebbles suggestive of a warm maritime location

Top right, centre and right: Water sculpture can come in many forms and guises, from a monumental cactus bubble fountain by Alan and Terry Wilson to the humorous plug and zip pieces designed by Mark Richard Hall

Lighting and illusion

Water is essentially about light and reflection, so it is worth considering how these qualities can be further enhanced to add a touch of illusion and magic to your garden.

Mirrors

Water introduces a reflective light-catching surface that can be emphasized by using mirrors. A mirror can create an illusion of more space, but it needs to be carefully sited to avoid reflecting any unsightly element in the garden. Placing the mirror at an angle will prevent you from seeing your own reflection and create the illusion of a further space beyond the glass. This can be even more effective if a convincing surround such as a timber arch is used to hide the edges.

Above: **A mirror behind this waterfall enhances its reflective qualities**

Above right and right: **Setting a mirror at an angle to the viewer and concealing its edges behind a wrought-iron gate creates the illusion of a garden beyond, whereas a mirror set in a timber frame and continued below water level effectively doubles the size of a small garden**

Lighting

Lighting your pond or water feature will add to its appeal, enabling you to enjoy it into the evening. Provided you keep interior lights low you will even be able to appreciate it from inside the house. Lighting can almost create another garden, with a night version totally different in appearance and atmosphere to the daytime one.

It may be necessary to light your pond as a safety measure, and it is certainly a good idea to light stepping stones and bridges if the garden is to be used at night, but lighting need not only be functional. Underwater lighting can be placed beneath a deck or bridge to make the structure appear to float or it can graze up an adjacent wall to create rippling effects across the surface. An underwater light can be mounted beneath a waterfall to provide a spectacular effect, causing the falling water to glow. This, combined with the sound of the fall, introduces a real sense of theatre at night.

Illuminating a fountain will make the water droplets sparkle when seen against a dark background and lighting waterside features, such as sculpture or specimen plants, doubles their effect as they reflect in the water below. A spotlight can also be directed at fountain features such as wall-mounted spouts and bubbling urns to draw focal points out of the darkness.

Lighting should be designed to provide a subtle and magical effect, so restraint is the watchword. However, it is important to light both the pond and supporting elements around to create a complete night-time picture. Remember that it is the lighting effect you want to see, not the light source, so try to keep the light fittings as unobtrusive as

possible (many are finished in matt black or copper verdigris to help in this respect). Finally, do not ignore the possibilities of simpler options such as garden torches and candles, perhaps in combination with more permanent lighting, to create a magical atmosphere.

Left: **An antique wellhead above the source of a rill has been lit in order to double its impact as it reflects in the water below**

Left: **A spotlight on a spilling urn water feature makes it a focal point at night**

Useful tips

• Try out possible lighting effects with powerful torches to assess their impact from various viewpoints around the garden, but avoid any direct contact with water

• Simple white lights are more restful than coloured ones as they allow the natural colours of the lit objects to show through

3 • Water Garden Design

Once you have considered all the design choices available (see pages 14–31) you will be in a position to select the most appropriate type of pond or water feature to suit both you and your garden. Whether you opt for a raised or sunken pond, a stream or a self-contained fountain, it will inevitably become a focus in the garden and so its style and location within the wider setting are paramount. Mistakes can be expensive or impossible to rectify later, so careful planning at the outset is essential.

Siting your pond

The location of your pond will be determined by its relationship to the house, the garden boundaries and existing features such as trees, as well as general site conditions such as slopes and shelter. These factors may also affect the type of feature it is possible to install. Furthermore, you must consider its siting relative to all the other elements of your garden such as the terrace, lawn, paths and planting. It is unlikely there

will be the perfect place, but by juggling with all the issues and thinking of the site as a whole, a pond can be positioned in the best location that your particular garden and specific requirements will allow.

Practical considerations

Before excavating your pond it is essential to establish the position of any underground services (gas pipes, electric cables, drains, soakaways and sewers) so that they can be avoided. You should also site your pond far enough from trees and boundaries to avoid damage to roots and foundations.

Slope, drainage and soil Gardens are rarely completely level and where possible a pond should be located at a low point. This not only looks and feels right but surface water run off will help keep the pond topped up naturally. Sloping sites allow for the creation of moving water features in the form of streams, rills and waterfalls.

Underlying rock, soil type and drainage patterns will also influence the siting and type of pond. Hard rock close to the surface can be difficult and expensive to excavate and you may choose to install a raised pond to avoid having to do this. A high water table or poorly drained ground can also cause a problem in that water in the ground exerts pressure from below that can damage the pond structure. Flexible liners can balloon up, a phenomenon known as 'hippo-ing' for obvious reasons. On ground of this nature the only solution is to install a drainage system beneath the liner to remove the excess water.

Below: **The change of level in this country garden has been exploited to create a raised stone pond with spillways. The rounded shape of the pond reflects the curving line of the retaining wall and the same stone has been used for both to make for a cohesive design**

Left: This informal pond is located in the lowest part of the garden from where a view to open countryside can be enjoyed

BE AWARE

● Beware of run off from fertilized beds and lawns, driveways and other polluted surfaces entering the pond and affecting its natural balance

● Still water is highly reflective so avoid locating the pond where the water surface will cause glare or reflect unsightly aspects of the garden or of a building, such as drainpipes

● The removal of excavated pond spoil can be expensive, so consider how this can be reused in the garden

Sun, shade and shelter A pond should be located in a bright, open site that ideally receives some shade for at least part of the day. Too much sun will increase evaporation rates and the tendency for algae (green water) to proliferate; too much shade will limit the range of aquatic plants that can be grown and reduce the ability of the pond to support life. Shade from walls is preferable to that cast by overhanging trees as falling leaves cause a problem.

In exposed sites ponds suffer from increased evaporation, both from the water itself and through the leaves of plants that take up more water from the pond to compensate. A pond located in a sheltered site is also more attractive to wildlife and preferable for pond plants, many of which have tall stems that can be damaged by high winds.

Wind will also disrupt fountain effects, causing water loss as well as creating unpleasant rushes of water from spouts and falls rather than the steady relaxing sound they are designed to make. Exposed sites can be made more sheltered by hedges or windbreaks that will benefit the whole garden as well as the pond.

Right: Sited close to the house, this pond acts as a division between a decked terrace and the rest of the garden

Aesthetic considerations

A pond can be any size, shape or style as long as it is keyed into its location and in scale with its surroundings. As water is such a powerful visual element, any pond or water feature must be carefully placed in order to balance the garden scene. You must consider where it will be viewed from and what it will be seen against.

Siting the pond close to the house can bring the enjoyment of water indoors. Dark interiors can be brightened by the reflection of light on water and where moving water is present beautiful rippling effects can be created on walls and ceilings. At night, a lit pond can be a real feature seen from inside. Remember too that the sound of water can create a relaxing background.

A good backdrop is essential to the success of a pond or water feature. Water maximizes the effect of its surroundings, so consider locating the pond to make the most of any features worth

Above: A framework of carefully chosen plants integrates this fountain feature into its setting

reflecting, such as planting groups or attractive architectural features. Bear in mind that the best reflections are achieved when the backdrop is lit and the sun is behind the viewer.

Below: This formal pond has been located to reflect the regular façade of the house

Above: In this formal garden a slate-edged rill has been designed to reflect a majestic oak tree in the water along its length

Above: The pond in this small formal garden is designed to be enjoyed from the adjoining loggia

Themed water gardens

A pond or water feature should always be designed as an integral part of the overall garden composition and styled accordingly. On the following pages a water feature has been incorporated into different garden settings in order to demonstrate how water can enhance a garden and how a garden can be styled so that it harmonizes with the water feature.

Each section begins by showing an existing water feature in a town garden, a city garden or a tiny space, followed by a number of alternative designs for the same size of site.

Above: This circular raised brick pond is keyed into its location, being concentric to the enclosing wall and constructed from the same material

Above: Framed with planting and positioned at the end of a vista, a wall-mounted fountain makes a real focal point

Town Gardens

BE AWARE

◉ Only consider creating an area of open water when your children are old enough to be aware of the dangers

◉ A boundary hedge of fast-growing conifers will make you more aware of the limits of your garden and will soon shade out both you and your neighbours

Above: A red water lily provides a cheerful spot of colour in the garden pond

The garden is increasingly being seen as an outdoor room in which to play, dine, entertain and generally relax as well as providing a means of expressing individuality and creativity. Whatever your requirements and tastes, the ideas in this section will act as inspiration and can be adapted to suit any size or shape of garden in town or country.

Design considerations

Town gardens are often large enough to cater for a whole range of activities and can be designed in a variety of ways. The architecture of your house and the location of your garden within the wider landscape are important factors to be taken into account. Providing a degree of privacy is also important, but try to resist delineating your plot with a line of fast-growing conifers in an attempt to screen it from the neighbours. Instead, plant a carefully located tree and a mix of shrubs, grasses and perennials. The varying heights, shapes, colours and textures will not only disguise the boundaries but will also create a greater sense of mystery and make the garden feel larger.

Water in the garden

Provided you allow sufficient space for functional requirements such as seating and dining areas, access, storage and screening, you can include a sizeable area of water – perhaps a large wildlife pond, for instance. If you have a young family, however, you may prefer to install a safe water feature instead and devote more of the garden to play areas and lawn.

Above: A drilled boulder fountain within this pond provides extra interest with sound and movement as well as aerating the water

The decked water garden

In the town garden opposite, the pond is the focus and takes the place of the traditional lawn. The reflection of the sky and the surrounding plants makes the garden feel much larger and brighter. Smart timber decking close to the house creates a generous space for dining and entertaining and a carefully placed tree provides shade and privacy. A matching boardwalk leads off to the rest of the garden. Tall, lush grasses, fine-leaved bamboos and bold-leaved moisture-loving plants disguise the boundaries and soften the straight lines of the rectangular design.

Right: Within this small town garden the principal elements of water, timber decking and lush naturalistic planting combine to create a pleasing asymmetrical composition

BE AWARE

● Bamboos can be invasive and puncture pond liners, so use clump-forming species or plant them in containers

● Koi have very exacting requirements but colour and movement can be achieved instead with less demanding golden orfe and goldfish

Right: Stepping stones lead to a timber teahouse. Pines, bamboos, Japanese maples and irises frame the view

The oriental look

Maybe you aspire to a garden of peace, tranquillity and hidden depth that reveals itself to you slowly. Using the same plot and with roughly the same proportion of open water, you can create an oriental-style garden. Japanese gardens are ideally suited to smaller spaces as they often represent an entire landscape in miniature, with, for instance, rocks placed in water to represent islands and pebble 'beaches' becoming shorelines.

The key to this look is simplicity and attention to detail. Avoid cluttering the space with competing elements and garish colours. Choose natural materials such as stone and timber for surfaces and structures and use the subtle textures and shades of green of bamboos, grasses and evergreen shrubs. Splashes of colour will appear throughout the year from cherries, azaleas, Japanese irises and the autumn leaves of Japanese maples, while fish in your pond will provide both colour and movement.

Traditional Japanese artefacts such as water basins (*tsukubai*), deer scarers

Above: A *tsukubai* was traditionally used for washing the hands as part of the Japanese Tea Ceremony

(*shishi-odoshi*) and stone lanterns are essential to create the oriental look and must be carefully placed in the garden setting. Because of their strong character you will need only one or two pieces to create the right atmosphere, allowing you to choose authentic items made from natural stone without incurring too much expense. Remember that you can exploit the reflective qualities of still, open water to double the value of your plants and ornamental features.

1 **REFLECTING POND** An informal pond provides a home for fish and a surface that reflects Japanese artefacts and surrounding plants

2 **PEBBLE BEACH** A gently shelving pebble 'beach' provides an attractive edge to the pond and disguises the liner

3 **TIMBER STAKES** Short stakes are used to edge the pool and contain marginal plants such as the Japanese iris (*Iris laevigata*)

4 **BRIDGE** This timber bridge has a zigzag design that is believed to deter evil spirits which can only move in straight lines

5 **STEPPING STONES** Carefully spaced stones slow the pace so that the various aspects of the garden can be fully appreciated

6 **WATER BASIN** A *tsukubai* provides the restful sound of trickling water and is lit by a traditional stone lantern

7 **STONE LANTERN** The lantern is set on a promontory to reflect in the water; a candle would give a magical touch at night

8 **FEATURE ROCK** A carefully placed rock in the pond represents an island in miniature

9 **BAMBOOS** These are essential plants for the Japanese garden and can be pruned to accentuate attractive stems such as those of the black bamboo (*Phyllostachys nigra*)

10 **BAMBOO SCREENS** Bamboo fencing or panels attached to the boundary provide an authentic backdrop

11 **GATE** An oriental-style gate suggests that the theme continues beyond the boundaries

12 **CONTAINERS** Stone or glazed pots can be planted with plantain lilies (*Hosta* sp.) and Japanese maples such as *Acer palmatum* 'Dissectum Atropurpureum', especially if your soil is unsuitable for these typically oriental plants

Key features

- Timeless materials (brick, stone or modern reproductions)

- Symmetrical layout and geometric shapes

- Axial lines, framed views and focal points

- Mixed planting of shrubs, perennials and clipped plants

- Formal reflecting ponds for lilies and fish

- Raised ponds, rills and fountains

BE AWARE

- Sunken ponds can be dangerous for children; raised ponds are safer and look equally good in formal garden layouts

- Fish ponds are ideally suited to formal gardens but make sure the filtration system is concealed

Right: **Built-in furniture needs to be integrated into the design. Here a slate fountain doubles as a wine cooler and table**

The traditional look

If your tastes are more traditional or you live in a period house and would like a garden to match, the same plot can be given a more orderly, formal look. By basing a design about an axis and employing shapes, lines, proportions and materials to reflect those used for the house you can achieve an integrated composition. Water can be contained within formal rills and pools, perhaps with fountains as central features.

The key to the traditional look is symmetry and order. Even if you have existing features or an irregularly shaped plot that might suggest a more asymmetric design, your garden can still be balanced and controlled. Terraces, lawns and pools should be geometric in shape and contained within paths, edging strips or planting beds. Pots and ornaments should be placed centrally, symmetrically or at the ends of vistas to act as focal points.

Traditional materials for surfaces and structures will usually be brick or stone, laid in regular, geometric patterns or

Above: **The formality of this classical urn and supporting pedestal is softened with abundant planting**

contained within a regular framework or contrasting edging material. As the planting is also contained it can be made more informal in appearance with a mix of shrubs and perennials, but some clipped plants can be included as focal points. Allow plants to spill over onto adjacent surfaces for a romantic look or edge the borders with low hedging, such as box (*Buxus* sp.), for a crisper finish.

1 SUNKEN POND A slate-edged rectangular fishpond is centrally located and formally planted with marginal plants and water lilies

2 WALL FOUNTAIN A wall-mounted fountain provides a focal point at the end of the central axis

3 RILL A narrow slate-edged channel takes water from the wall fountain to the pond. The moving water helps to oxygenate the pond, making it more habitable for fish

4 BRICK PAVING Brick is laid in a regular basket-weave pattern around the pool and on the terrace. It contrasts well with the slate edgings and stone flags

5 STONE PAVING Traditional stone flags are used to surface the terrace. Their dimensions determine the size of the area so that no flags need be cut to fit

6 STEPPING STONES Stone flags surrounded with pebbles provide a subtle division between the terrace and the rest of the garden

7 BUILT-IN FURNITURE A slate-topped bench and table fitted with a flat fountain provide a focus to the terrace

8 SLATE BENCH A bench is located on the cross axis of the pond and set back into the planting so as not to restrict access

9 BOUNDARY WALLS The boundaries have been painted a terracotta colour to match the brick surfacing, bench and table bases and to set off the planting

10 FORMAL PLANTS Box plants, clipped into cones, frame the focal point at the end of the garden and provide formal accents in the borders

11 MIXED PLANTING A variety of shrubs, grasses and perennials are contained within formally shaped borders

12 CONTAINERS Square containers give this traditional layout a more contemporary feel. They are regularly spaced and formally planted and are repeated further down the garden

Key features

• Soft materials (grass, bark, sand) for safe landings

• Safe, secure boundaries and structures

• A practical, simple layout and well-laid surfaces

• A safe reservoir water feature for younger children

• A wildlife pond with shallow sides for older children

• Storage space for bicycles and toys

BE AWARE

● Lawn can become damaged with excessive use, so choose a durable grass mix and do not mow the lawn too short

● Keep spiky and prickly plants away from play areas and avoid poisonous and irritant plants such as spurges (*Euphorbia* sp.)

● Small children can drown in as little as 5 cm (2 in) of water, so install a safe fountain feature or place a grille over any open water

The family garden

If you have children your garden is one of your greatest assets and the same plot can be replanned for family use. Children can spend hours outside, releasing plenty of physical and creative energy in playing games, climbing trees, building hideaways and messing about with sand and water. Of course open water is a hazard to young children and you may prefer to install a safe water feature with a concealed reservoir. Older children will delight in a wildlife pond, however, so plan ahead and consider where one might fit later.

The key to a successful family garden is flexibility. It must cater for all ages and interests and be able to adapt over time as children grow up. Your garden can be any style as long as it is practical and able to withstand a certain amount of wear without looking too damaged. Choose a simple, informal layout that allows children to move around freely and make sure that surfaces are safe and boundaries secure. Plants should be tough and able to recover quickly if they are damaged.

Above: **A winding tunnel, too small for adults, is easy and inexpensive to make from woven willow stems**

Some lawn for playing ball games and pitching tents will be appreciated, as will climbing structures, swings and possibly a small plot in which to grow plants. Young children enjoy sandpits, which you may wish to site close to the house where they can be seen, while older children prefer their own private space in which to be creative and adventurous.

Below: **A large millstone over an enclosed underground reservoir creates a safe water feature for young children to have fun with**

1 SANDPIT Surrounded by small log seats and tough plants, a sandpit located close to the house can easily be converted to a pond as children grow older

2 GEYSER FOUNTAIN A fountain set in cobbles allows children to enjoy playing with water without any danger of drowning

3 SHALLOW STREAM Fed by the fountain and covered with rounded pebbles, a shallow stream is great fun for paddling and sailing paper boats. The water is recycled from a concealed reservoir

4 WIGWAM A simple structure made from timber poles provides a secret hideaway for older children

5 LAWN Grass is a soft, practical surface for children to play on. It is edged with timber blocks to make mowing easier

6 BENCH A simple bench made from an old tree provides a place to sit and enjoy the garden

7 BOUNDARIES A strong timber fence and a gate fitted with childproof latches provide a secure boundary to the garden

8 STEPPING STONES As well as providing access, log sections laid in the ground are great for jumping and skipping between

9 SWING Trees with strong limbs can be used to hang a swing from and a bark surface beneath allows for a soft landing

10 CONTAINERS Half barrels can be used to create mini ponds until a wildlife pond can be installed

11 PICNIC TABLE Inexpensive wooden picnic tables with built-in benches are ideal for young children prone to tipping over on conventional seats

12 BUILT-IN BARBECUE Cooking and eating outside creates a holiday environment for the whole family

Key features

- Natural materials (stone, timber, gravel)

- A shallow-edged pond with pebble beach and marsh

- Native (or near-native) trees, shrubs and wildflowers

- Nectar-rich and berry-bearing plants

- Blurred divisions between habitats

- A nettle patch in an out-of-the-way corner for butterfly larvae

---

BE AWARE

● Avoid chemicals and let birds, frogs and beneficial insects control garden pests in an organic and sustainable way

● Native plants attract native wildlife and are consequently more beneficial than most ornamental plants

● Avoid any disruption during the hibernating, nesting and breeding seasons

The habitat garden

With the increasing demands made on land for housing, industry and agriculture, gardens are becoming important refuges for displaced wildlife. The traditional habitats of woodland, wetland and meadow are being lost and wild plants and creatures are under threat. If you are keen to redress the balance, with the added benefit of natural pest control, you can design, plant and manage your garden especially for wildlife. The same plot can be reworked as a habitat garden for birds, butterflies, amphibians and mammals.

The key to a successful wildlife garden is the re-creation of the habitats found in nature on a smaller scale. The design need not be informal in style, although softer lines and less structural edges allow adjoining habitats to merge more easily. You can mimic woodland by planting a hedge or a tree, some native shrubs and a groundcover of woodland wildflowers, bulbs and ferns.

Above: Greater knapweed (*Centaurea scabiosa*) is a rich source of nectar for bees and butterflies. The mown grass edge to the meadow shows that the garden is well tended

A grassland habitat can be an area of grass kept longer or a mini wildflower meadow cut once or twice a year. Making a pond to re-create a wetland habitat is essential; ideally a bog or marsh will be included too (see pages 62–7, 100–1).

Complement the design with natural materials and supplement the habitats with fruiting shrubs for birds and nectar plants for bees and butterflies. Bird and bat boxes, stones and log piles are all beneficial additions.

Left: Creating a wildlife pond surrounded with native plants and wildflowers is the best contribution you can make to wildlife conservation in the garden

1 **WILDLIFE POND** An informal pond with shallow margins provides a habitat for dragonflies and amphibians as well as native pond plants such as yellow flag (*Iris pseudacorus*) and marsh plants such as purple loosestrife (*Lythrum salicaria*)

2 **PEBBLE BEACH** This gently shelving edge allows safe and easy access for amphibians as well as birds and mammals that come to drink

3 **BRIDGE** A timber boardwalk allows close observation of pond life and provides access to the rest of the garden

4 **WILDFLOWER MEADOW** This provides a rich source of nectar for insects and adjoins the woodland edge and pond to provide a continuous undisturbed habitat

5 **MOWN GRASS** This allows access to a bird table and keeps the edge of the meadow looking neat and tidy

6 **WOODLAND EDGE** Native and berry-bearing shrubs are underplanted with woodland wildflowers to create a habitat for birds and mammals

7 **MIXED HEDGE** A hedge of mixed native plants creates a sheltered habitat and wildlife corridor

8 **TIMBER FENCE** A fence provides a simple backdrop to the garden and is clothed in nectar-rich climbing plants such as honeysuckle (*Lonicera* sp.)

9 **COMPOST BINS** Garden waste is recycled and incorporated back into the garden system. The bins are hidden behind evergreen shrubs

10 **LOG PILE** Surrounded by woodland wildflowers, this offers a shady home for beetles and insects which in turn provide food for birds and mammals

11 **NECTAR BORDER** Butterfly bush (*Buddleia davidii*), ice plants (*Sedum spectabile*), lavenders (*Lavandula* sp.) and herbs boost nectar supplies

12 **FURNITURE AND POTS** Simple timber furniture and containers placed on a gravel terrace reflect the quiet natural harmony of the wildlife garden

Design focus

- The sound of moving water soothes the senses and counteracts traffic noise

- Open water reflects the sky and brings light down into the space

- Good-quality furniture that can be left outside all year saves on precious storage space

- Lighting will enhance the garden at night from inside as well as out

BE AWARE

● In confined spaces there is a fine line between the soothing sound of trickling water and the irritating noise of constant splashing

● Avoid lawn in gardens of this size as it will wear out too quickly and space will be required to store the mower

● If your only access is through the house, material size and machinery will be limited by the size of your doors

City Gardens

As pressures on urban living become more intense, the need for somewhere to escape the bustle and connect with nature becomes more important. A city garden need only be the size of a large room to become a place of retreat and escapism. Whatever the dimensions and location of your garden, the ideas in this section can be incorporated or adapted.

Design considerations

City spaces are often overlooked, overshadowed and overheard, but with some careful planning such problems can be overcome or turned to your advantage. You may not be able to hide all the unattractive views beyond the boundaries, but providing a better one within them will direct your eye to something more appealing. With no need to worry about keeping in harmony with the surroundings, the garden you create can be pure fantasy. As space is at a premium each plant and feature must earn its keep, but in a limited area good-quality materials are affordable.

Water in the garden

As long as you allow enough space for sitting out and enjoying the garden the rest can be devoted to plants and water. Lawn is not really an option in a small city garden but a water feature can easily be accommodated. It will cool and brighten the space and any splashing or trickling sound will counteract the constant hum of traffic.

Left: The fern-like mosaics on this concrete pond complement the linear foliage of the irises

Above: A smooth sheet of water spills between two ponds and adds a sense of drama to the garden, especially when lit from below at night

The obelisk water garden

In the city courtyard opposite, a split-level pond topped with an obelisk provides the backdrop to a terrace large enough for alfresco dining. A smooth sheet of water spills from a central raised pool into a lower canal running the width of the garden. Materials and detailing are carefully co-ordinated. Slate is used to pave the terrace and edge the raised pond and fine mosaic work on the wall is reflected on the tabletop. The effect is one of crisp and controlled formality softened with lush and textural planting. This is not a garden for children but for busy, stylish urbanites.

Right: A split-level pond and central waterfall enlivens and cools this city garden. The formality of the design is reinforced by the classical obelisk and symmetrical planting

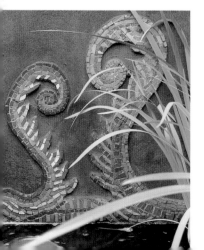

The tropical look

If you like big plants with big impact you can create a tropical-style garden in the same plot and use the level change to make a 'natural' waterfall. Small city spaces are ideally suited to this style of garden. The warmer microclimate and often shadier conditions in built-up areas are ideal for growing more exotic plants, while large plants with huge leaves look particularly jungly when grown together in confined spaces.

The key to the tropical look is the combination of foliage shapes and textures to create the impression of luxuriant growth. Grow subtropical plants with strong form such as palms and bananas to provide an overhead canopy. Combine these with the lacy fronds of primeval tree ferns and finely cut foliage of bamboos and grasses. A framework of hardy, exotic-looking evergreens such as *Fatsia japonica*,

Above: Tender *Canna indica* can be combined with hardy plants such as *Hosta* 'Halcyon' and *Fatsia japonica* to create a tropical look

magnolia and laurel will maintain interest throughout the year, and shade-tolerant groundcovers and vibrantly coloured flowers will complete the composition. A pond will cool the scene, humidify the atmosphere and allow you to grow exciting tropical water plants. Consider installing an automatic irrigation system to mist the garden and mimic rainforest conditions.

Natural materials such as water-worn rock and timber decking can be used for structures and surfaces. Boundaries can be clad in reed panels and covered with trumpet vines (*Campsis* sp.) and passionflowers (*Passiflora* sp.). Glazed pots, rattan chairs, an earthenware barbecue and a table set for cocktails will transport you to far-flung tropical places.

Left: Tropical water lilies and *Cyperus papyrus* are essential water plants for the tropical pond

1 POND AND WATERFALL A rock-edged pond fed by a 'natural' waterfall cools and humidifies the atmosphere for plants and aerates the water for fish

2 POND PLANTS Tropical water lilies and tender marginal plants such as the arum lily (*Zantedeschia aethiopica*) and papyrus (*Cyperus papyrus*) can be overwintered in deeper parts of the pond

3 PALMS These provide an overhead canopy and an instant sense of the tropics. The chusan palm (*Trachycarpus fortunei*) is hardy in temperate climates

4 HUGE LEAVES Bananas (*Musa basjoo*), foxglove trees (*Paulownia tomentosa*) and cannas are essential exotics for the protected tropical garden

5 FINE LEAVES The foliage of bamboos and grasses provides a contrast to the huge leaves of other plants in the tropical garden

6 TREE FERNS Shade, shelter and humidity are required for growing tree ferns (*Dicksonia antarctica*) and winter protection will be necessary

7 GROUNDCOVERS Ferns and plantain lilies (*Hosta* sp.) benefit from the shade and humid atmosphere of dense planting

8 FLOWER COLOUR Hardy plants with exotic-looking flowers such as montbretia (*Crocosmia* sp.) and day lilies (*Hemerocallis* sp.) provide bright splashes of colour. More tender plants such as lobelias, salvias and verbenas can be grown as annuals

9 TIMBER DECKING Decking is warm underfoot and implies that the garden has been made from materials of the forest. It can be cut around rocky outcrops and given a more rounded, informal edge

10 POTS AND CONTAINERS Colourful glazed pots can be planted with exotics such as cannas and ginger lilies (*Hedychium* sp.) or even indoor plants brought outside for the summer

11 REED PANELS Boundaries can be fitted with reed screens to provide a suitably tropical backdrop

BE AWARE

● Moving water helps keep the pond aerated, but without plants to keep it clear the use of chemicals may be necessary

● Make sure that the sound of moving water is not too disturbing and contrary to the notion of a minimalist retreat

● Stone, glass and steel can be costly, but in small spaces with less surface area to cover more expensive materials can be afforded

The minimalist look

If your tastes are more contemporary and you aspire to a minimalist look, the same plot can be reworked. The level change can still be used to exploit the sound of falling water but can be given a more modernist interpretation. Minimalist gardens are the perfect antidote to busy city lifestyles, providing you with a cool, tranquil space that requires very little of your time to maintain.

The key to the minimalist look is the paring back to only that which is essential. All extraneous clutter should be removed so that the clarity of the composition can be contemplated. Combine pure forms, clean lines and minimal colours to create a sense of balance and proportion and make sure that all the ingredients (materials, plants, water and furniture) work towards this aim.

Modernist materials such as concrete, steel and glass are suited to the look, although any material used in a crisp, clean manner can be minimalist. Cut, sawn and polished stone is particularly suitable for floors if your budget will stretch. Planting will add colour and softness to the space, but try to limit your selection: a single plant with a strong shape can look stunning seen against a bare wall, especially when illuminated at night. Water should be used in a crisp, sculptural way. Rills, canals, fountains and still, open water are all appropriate provided the effect is bold and simple.

Right: **The smooth clean lines and surfaces of stone, decking, steel and glass complement this modernist water feature**

Above: **The vertical form of maiden grass *Miscanthus sinensis* 'Gracillimus' is contrasted with the crisp horizontal line of a steel pond edge**

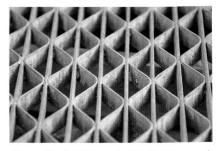

Above: **Steel grilles make ideal bridges and walkways in a minimalist garden**

① **WATER** The sensual effect of water is all around. A narrow canal punctuated with fountains and edged with steel wraps around three sides of the terrace

② **WALL FOUNTAINS** Regularly spaced stainless steel pipes spill water into the canal from ascending heights along the angled retaining wall.

③ **BUBBLE FOUNTAINS** Set at regular intervals along the length of two sides of the canal, bubble fountains break the surface and send out ripples

④ **BRIDGE** A steel grille placed across the canal allows access from the house to the terrace. Its size and shape correspond to paving slab dimensions

⑤ **RETAINING WALL** The concrete wall behind the fountains has been angled to add an exciting dimension to the garden

⑥ **STONE PAVING** Smooth, square limestone slabs laid in a simple grid pattern create a clean, uncluttered and minimalist surface

⑦ **BAMBOOS** The black stems of *Phyllostachys nigra* make a striking contrast with the pale concrete walls and provide a low-maintenance evergreen backdrop. Its rustling leaves help to counteract the constant hum of traffic

⑧ **GRASSES** The soft foliage of *Miscanthus sinensis* and other tall grasses complements the hard lines of the design. A limited plant palette has been used for maximum impact

⑨ **SEDGES** Low sedges provide an ever-green strip of colour between the canal and angled wall. The splashing fountains create a constantly moist environment

⑩ **FURNITURE** Stylish modern furniture complements the look and acts as a piece of sculpture in its own right

⑪ **BOUNDARY WALLS** These have been finished with a cement render to provide a smooth, clean and minimalist backdrop to the garden

Key features

- Formal raised ponds with cooling fountains

- Natural materials (stone, pebbles, terracotta, timber)

- Scented flowers and aromatic foliage

- Vertical and clipped evergreen plants such as cypress (*Cupressus* sp.) and box (*Buxus* sp.)

- Silver and grey foliage (olives and lavenders)

- Terracotta pots of agapanthus, agaves and citrus plants

BE AWARE

- A raised water feature is ideal where excavation for a sunken pond is impossible

- Tender plants may need to be brought inside over winter, which is easy if they are planted in movable pots

- Mediterranean herbs such as lavender and sage (*Salvia officinalis*) need to be trimmed over to keep them bushy

The Mediterranean look

Another approach for the same plot would be to create a sensual garden evocative of the Mediterranean. The level change can be utilized, perhaps by allowing water to spill from a spout into a raised stone trough, as you might find in a Provençale village. Many of the plants grown in regions around the world with Mediterranean climates are perfectly hardy in warm city gardens provided they receive enough sunlight. However, this style of garden is difficult to create in dark, damp spaces because you need the right sun-loving plants to evoke the mood.

Below: **Terracotta pots planted with tender agaves and olives are essential features in a Mediterranean-style garden**

Above: **The pretty little rock plant *Erigeron karvinskianus* froths around a clipped box ball and spills over onto a pebble path**

The key to the Mediterranean look is warm, natural materials, combined with soft, textural, often aromatic planting. Allow materials to weather naturally and paint to peel and fade. Plants can tumble over hard edges, scramble up walls and over rustic structures and self-seed into cracks and crevices. The effect you are aiming for is one of untended charm.

For walls and surfaces use warm stone and terracotta or concrete, rendered and whitewashed or painted in soft, chalky colours. Timber poles can be bound together to create structures for climbing plants such as wisteria, vines (*Vinifera* sp.) and heavily scented jasmine (*Jasminum* sp.). Structural plants such as olives (*Olea europaea*), palms, figs (*Ficus* sp.) and cypresses (*Cupressus* sp.) can be underplanted with lavenders (*Lavandula* sp.), bearded irises and culinary herbs. Alfresco dining is essential to Mediterranean life and this style of garden should inspire you to eat, drink and entertain outside.

1 RAISED POND Reminiscent of a large drinking trough or communal washing place, a formal raised pond is fed by stone water-spouts and faced in honey-coloured stone

2 OLIVE TREES The gnarled trunks and silver foliage of *Olea europaea* evoke an image of Mediterranean landscapes. They will need to be protected over winter

3 ITALIAN CYPRESSES The vertical forms of *Cupressus sempervirens* lead the eye upwards and are strongly associated with Mediterranean regions

4 LAVENDERS The rounded forms of these essential sun-loving plants hug the ground and compliment the vertical forms of cypress and iris

5 HERBS Culinary plants such as rosemary (*Rosmarinus officinalis*), sage and thyme (*Thymus* sp.) provide flavourings to Mediterranean cooking and a scented atmosphere in which to dine alfresco

6 TERRACOTTA TILES These are a natural choice to surface this style of garden and the warm earth tones of terracotta reduce the glare from the sun

7 PEBBLE MOSAIC Pebbles set in mortar is a very Mediterranean detail and can be used as a contrasting texture in the garden

8 POTS Terracotta pots and classical urns are essential. They can be plain, decoratively carved or painted, and planted with tender agaves and agapanthus

9 CITRUS FRUITS Oranges and lemons can be grown in pots and moved to frost-free quarters over winter

10 FURNITURE Simple, rustic timber furniture, painted blue to contrast with terracotta, will age attractively over time when allowed to weather naturally

11 CLIMBING PLANTS Jasmine, wisteria and vines grown over walls and rustic supports blur the boundaries and provide just the right touch of rambling informality

Below: A reclaimed slate ridge tile is inverted to make an ingenious spillway

Tiny Spaces

With a little thought and ingenuity even the smallest of spaces can be transformed by the addition of water. Whether you have a basement or balcony, passageway or patio, the ideas in this section can be adapted to fit or even incorporated into the design for a much larger garden.

Design considerations

You may not spend time in your tiny space, but if you walk through it or look out onto it every day it probably impacts on you more than you realize. In tiny spaces vertical surfaces are important and can be enhanced with paint, trellis or climbing plants. Mirrors can be employed to deceive the eye and make the space seem larger, and garden lighting can bring an extra dimension at night.

Water in the garden

There may not be room to install a pond but you can easily add a water feature as long as you leave enough space for access. Still or falling water will brighten a space by reflecting light, and fountains will enliven it with sound and movement. Self-contained fountain features take up very little room and wall-mounted fountains are particularly space-efficient. Small containers can be filled with water to create mini ponds. Whatever water feature you choose to install, it should complement and be enhanced by its surroundings.

The reclaimed water feature

In the small space opposite a water feature has been designed to reflect the layout and recycled theme of the garden

Above: The water spilling from this reclaimed tin bathtub is recycled via a pump concealed in the grille-covered reservoir. Brick rubble completes the salvaged look

in which it sits. Reclaimed materials are combined to create a small, chunky fountain full of character. A spout made from a slate ridge tile is fed from a pipe concealed within a stack of concrete blocks. Water spills down onto a slate cube and over the edges of a slate slab into an underground reservoir, the sloping surfaces of swimming-pool edging units directing the water below ground. Second-hand granite setts edge the feature and reinforce the square theme, repeated again in the use of square trellis on the boundary fence. Low planting of varying colours and textures supports the feature and completes the composition.

Right: This simple water feature is made from reclaimed materials, skilfully combined and softened with planting, to create a delightful composition in a tiny corner space

Sea-washed timbers

Any mood or atmosphere can be created when all the ingredients work together to the same end. In this instance the same tiny space has been given a maritime theme with a water feature made from reclaimed timbers, reminiscent of coastal breakwaters. Each timber has been fitted with a hidden pipe that delivers water to small lengths of chain from where it drips down into a reservoir concealed beneath beach pebbles. A timber surround provides a surface on which to display the findings from beachcombing expeditions. The boundaries of the space have been concealed behind beach hut-style weather-boarding painted with chalky, sea-bleached colours. The supporting plants are all species associated with seaside environments such as grasses, sea hollies (*Eryngium* sp.) and thrift (*Armeria maritima*).

Above: Old railway sleepers placed vertically into the ground can evoke a seaside atmosphere when combined with gravel, pebbles and sea holly

Above: Ammonite sculptures arranged on a weathered timber deck strike a suitably maritime note

Reflected minimalism

In this design for the same corner space the theme is reflection. A shallow rectangular metal pan, brimming with water, brings light down into the space. A mirror is mounted on the rear boundary to double the effect of water and light, further brightening the space and making it appear much longer. Water issues from a large drilled stone and spills down into the pan, creating ripples across the surface (the spill can be seen in the mirrored image). An underground reservoir receives the water that spills over the sides and a pump recycles it back up through the stone. Minimal surface decoration and sculptural planting, with the emphasis on vertical form, completes the picture. An evergreen climbing plant conceals the edges of the mirror so as not to destroy the illusion.

Above: A large natural boulder drilled to take a bubbling fountain creates a feature with great presence, especially when combined with fine foliage

Above: The foliage of *Viburnum davidii* and bamboo (*Fargesia* sp.) combine to create a strong minimalist look

Contained exotica

Above: **This glazed plant container has been waterproofed to create a miniature lily pond**

A n exotic atmosphere has been created in the same space by a combination of glazed containers and luxuriant foliage. Ceramic containers make ideal water features where space is at a premium and especially where excavation for a pond may not be possible (see pages 60–1). In this design a glazed jar has been made into a bubbling fountain feature and acts as the focus of the composition. It has been grouped with two other glazed containers filled with water to create mini ponds, planted with tropical water plants. The water features have been arranged on a timber deck with cobbles around their base which also conceal the reservoir beneath the jar. A backdrop of reed fencing, tropical-looking foliage and brightly coloured flowers completes the arrangement.

Above: **Ceramic urns and jars fitted with overflowing fountains make delightful self-contained water features for patios, either placed singly or grouped**

Night-time elegance

Even in the daytime this clean-cut contemporary water feature would bring light and movement to the same tiny space, but at night it positively shimmers. A thread of water pours from a stainless steel spout mounted on the boundary wall and spills onto a slightly hollowed block of polished stone. It ripples across the surface of the stone and down the sides into a channel from where a concealed pump recycles the water back to the spout. At night all the falling water is lit from below. A carefully placed spotlight illuminates the narrow spill from the spout and further spots are positioned below the block to light the film of water spilling down the sides. Simple sculptural plants complete the composition. After dark they are also illuminated so as not to isolate the water feature from the rest of the night-time scene.

Above: Spotlights have been used to light the falling water from below and illuminate the copper façade of this contemporary water feature

Above: Plants with bold leaves and dramatic form such as the New Zealand flax (*Phormium* sp.) make ideal subjects for illumination

Container choice

• Reclaimed containers such as half barrels and stone troughs planted with native plants suit natural, informal gardens

• Stone and terracotta planters complement formal, traditional or Mediterranean-style gardens

• In oriental-style gardens, stone bowls planted with Japanese water plants are an ideal choice

• Glazed earthenware pots planted with tender plants suit tropical-style gardens

• Ceramic planters or fibreglass containers made to look like steel, copper or zinc complement more contemporary gardens

Below: **This old ceramic sink has been taken out of the kitchen and made into a container water garden. A small pump concealed in the sink recirculates the water through the tap**

Container water gardens

Where space for a pond is limited and excavation is impossible, for instance on roof gardens or verandahs and in conservatories, it is still possible to enjoy the qualities of water and grow pond plants. Ready-made containers intended for other purposes such as stone troughs, tubs and sinks, half barrels, large bowls, plant pots and urns can all be adapted to hold water and create mini ponds. They can either be fitted with a fountain for the sound of moving water or planted as a pond with floating-leaved, submerged and marginal plants.

Choosing the container

Choose your container to reflect the style of the garden. If it is not already watertight, a waterproof sealant should be applied to the inside and drainage holes in pots and planters should be plugged and sealed with a silicone sealant. If your container water garden is to stay outside over winter it must be strong enough to withstand freezing temperatures. Containers that are to be planted should be large enough to allow your chosen plants sufficient depth of water (see Plant Selector, pages 106–113).

Siting and planting

The beauty of container water gardens is that they are mobile, allowing you the flexibility to move them around to create changing garden pictures. As with siting a pond, the ideal location for a container water garden should be bright, sheltered and away from falling leaves, though providing sufficient shade for at least part of the day is important. This will

Above: **These stately blue-glazed pots planted with blue-flowered pickerel weed (*Pontaderia cordata*) make a strong impact**

lessen the temperature fluctuations associated with small volumes of shallow water and will also help to reduce water loss from the container through evaporation. Over winter, the container and its contents can be moved to a frost-free location or protected from low temperatures with bubble wrap, fleece or sacking.

Any aquatic plant can be grown in a container, including those that are highly invasive in garden ponds. Tender plants such as tropical water lilies (*Nymphaea* sp.) can also be grown, provided the container is brought into a greenhouse or conservatory over winter. As with a pond, submerged (oxygenating) plants will need to be included to keep the water clear and healthy. Planting in baskets within the container is also advisable as it keeps the growth of plants in check and allows easy maintenance.

Bog plants can also be grown in containers provided their needs for moisture and drainage are met. The growth of giant specimen plants such as *Gunnera manicata* can be restricted by planting them in a container, making them suitable for smaller gardens.

A half-barrel water garden

Old wooden barrels cut in half make ideal water gardens. If you are using an original half barrel make sure that it is still watertight and that no residues are present in the timbers. Clean the inside thoroughly and fill it with water to allow the timbers to expand and seal the container. Half barrel-style planters can also be used to create water gardens, but they may need to be coated with a proprietary sealant to make them watertight and to prevent preservatives in the timber from entering the water.

A 90 cm (3 ft) diameter half barrel will accommodate one water lily or floating-leaved plant, 3–5 marginal plants and 2–3 bunches of submerged (oxygenating) plants to keep the water clear. Free-floating plants can also be added. Plant each species in an aquatic planting basket (the submerged plants can be planted in a single basket), using well-sieved garden soil or aquatic compost, and cover each one with a

Above: A half barrel is large enough to accommodate miniature water lilies (*Nymphaea pygmaea* varieties) as well as the marginal dwarf bulrush (*Typha minima*)

1 cm (½ in) layer of gravel. Water each basket well and place it in the barrel, using bricks as necessary to raise each plant to its correct planting depth. Fill the barrel with water, preferably rainwater rather than tap water, and keep it topped up throughout the year. Thin and divide the plants as necessary.

> ### BE AWARE
>
> - Because of their restricted space and fluctuating water temperatures small containers are unsuitable for keeping fish
>
> - Water evaporates more quickly in small containers and so needs to be topped up more frequently
>
> - Plants in containers need to be divided more regularly than those in ponds to stop them overwhelming one another
>
> - The water in container gardens should not be allowed to freeze solid over winter as this will kill the plants

A PLANTED HALF BARREL

This half-barrel water garden is planted with predominantly native plants and would look well placed in a natural, informal setting

ARROWHEAD (*Sagittaria* sp.) provides structure and foliage interest

MINIATURE WATER LILIES provide surface shade and add flower colour

SUBMERGED PLANTS oxygenate the water and keep it clear and healthy

FLOWERING RUSH (*Butomus* sp.) provides height and vertical form as well as flower colour

AQUATIC PLANTING BASKETS restrain plant growth and make maintenance easier

BRICKS allow for a variety of planting depths for marginal and deeper water plants

Useful tips

- Placing the container on a platform with castors will allow it to be moved around more easily

- Grouping container water gardens increases moisture levels in the atmosphere to the benefit of all the aquatic plants

- Partially sinking the container into the ground will help regulate daily and seasonal temperature changes as well as offering some frost protection

4 • Creating a Wildlife Pond

Installing a pond is the most effective means of attracting wildlife into the garden and the best contribution you can make to nature conservation, going some way towards offsetting the dramatic loss of unpolluted wetland in the countryside. Shallow water is the greatest resource as most creatures live in the margins of ponds, lakes and watercourses and these are the conditions most closely mimicked by garden ponds. Frogs, toads and newts would be much rarer without garden ponds, as would diving-beetles, pond-skaters and damselflies which really benefit from such features. Ponds not only provide a home to these aquatic creatures but also attract birds and small mammals who will come to drink, feed and bathe. By creating a wildlife pond you have the chance to enjoy watching all these creatures close up without leaving your own home.

Above: **The garden wildlife pond provides a valuable home for the common frog (*Rana temporaria*), whose natural habitat is under threat**

NATIVE SHRUBS such as willow and dogwood offer valuable cover for birds and timid wildlife right up to the pond edge

A GARDEN SHED becomes a hide in which you can sit and watch the comings and goings of the wildlife pond at close quarters

MARGINAL PLANTS such as reeds and flag iris provide food and perches for insects and a refuge for pond-dwellers

FLOATING-LEAVED PLANTS such as water lilies give shade to help restrict the growth of algae as well as acting as landing pads for dragonflies and other insects

Siting the wildlife pond

If your main reason for establishing a pond in the garden is to attract as much wildlife as possible, its siting and design should be approached in a slightly different way than for a purely ornamental pond. It will still need to be sited in a sunny and sheltered part of the garden but its effect should be more subtle. Water always searches out the lowest ground, so if your aim is to mimic nature the pond will look more natural if it sits in a hollow or at the bottom of a slope.

Try not to isolate the pond from its immediate surroundings; think of it instead as part of a continuous habitat. It will be much more beneficial for timid wildlife if the water adjoins a marsh, a bog or long meadow grass and is protected by shrubs and trees, preferably species native to your region. You need to strike a balance between creating seclusion for the wildlife you want to attract and making the pond visible and accessible for you to enjoy. Provide a hard edge of paving, deck, pebbles or mown grass along one side to allow closer observation and the gentle pursuit of pond-dipping but make sure your children are aware of the dangers of water and are supervised at all times.

Above: In nature the division between water and dry land is gradual and you should aim to reproduce this continuous habitat in the garden

EXISTING TREES provide a natural woodland edge backdrop to the pond as well as nesting sites for birds and cover for other wildlife

A WILDFLOWER MEADOW adjacent to the pond increases its habitat value, encouraging even more insects for birds, bats and dragonflies

GENTLY SLOPING POND EDGES create a transition between open water and dry land, allowing easy access for frogs, toads and newts and for small mammals such as hedgehogs that come to drink

MOWN GRASS up to the pond edge allows you access to study the antics of pond skaters, water boatmen and all the other creatures in the wildlife pond

SUBMERGED OXYGENATING PLANTS keep the pond healthy and provide a refuge for pond creatures

Design focus

• If the lowest point of your garden is naturally wet, site the pond a little further up and create a bog garden lower down into which the pond can drain

BE AWARE

● Although nearby trees and shrubs are beneficial to wildlife, avoid locating your pond where roots and overhanging branches will cause problems

● Wildlife ponds are particularly attractive to children, who love to watch the activities of all the pond residents – but remember that open water is a hazard

Pond size, shape and profile

Above: **Close study of the comings and goings of pond life will engender in your children a respect for living things. A pebble edge affords safe and easy access for pond-dipping**

To maximize the number of visitors to your pond, aim for as large an expanse of water as your site and budget will allow. An ideal minimum size would be 4–5 m² (43–54 ft²), but a smaller pond will still attract a certain amount of interesting wildlife; an area of water only 1 m² (11 ft²) will be sufficient for frogs and common newts to breed, although toads and crested newts need more than 15 m² (161 ft²). If you have the space an informal shape will create a more natural look and maximize the length of valuable shoreline, but this is not essential. An adjacent wetland in the form of a marsh or bog garden (see pages 100–1) will provide another type of habitat, and in larger ponds an island will offer a safe haven.

Whatever the size of your pond, the important thing is to provide at least one gently sloping side to allow pond life easy access. Create plenty of soil-covered marginal shelves and areas of shallow water as these are the best habitats for most plants and animals. Aim for a saucer-shaped profile with a depth in the centre of at least 60 cm (2 ft), preferably 90 cm (3 ft). This will create a greater range of watery environments and prevent the pond from totally freezing in winter.

To achieve the preferred shape and profile, a flexible liner is the best method of containing the water. Preformed liners are often too small and shallow and do not readily lend themselves to soil planting shelves. The sides are often

A PROFILE OF THE WILDLIFE POND

A ROCK PILE provides amphibians with shade in summer and shelter in winter

LARGER STONES provide perches for birds and basking spots for amphibians

NATIVE FREE-FLOATING PLANTS give additional shade

NATIVE FLOATING-LEAVED PLANTS rooted in soil on the pond bottom shade the water and provide landing pads for insects

WETLAND PLANTS in planting pockets between pebbles give extra cover to wildlife

A SLOPING PEBBLE BEACH provides safe and easy access for amphibians, birds and small mammals

A FLEXIBLE LINER allows for a natural saucer-shaped profile and shallow edges

NATIVE SUBMERGED PLANTS rooted in soil maintain oxygen levels and provide shelter for pond creatures

Left: **A jetty projecting over the water allows you to watch the activities of the wildlife pond at close quarters**

Right: Dipping a net into the pond and studying the contents or bringing some pond water inside for closer observation (pond-dipping) can be fun for your children as well as educational. You may well find sticklebacks, toadspawn and frogspawn, underwater snails and newts

too steep to provide access for wildlife or escape for creatures that accidentally fall into the water, so if you do use a preformed liner make sure that some form of ramp is incorporated. Ponds in raised tubs and containers are also difficult for creatures to access and being small and shallow they are prone to rapid temperature fluctuations, heating up too much in summer and freezing in winter. This can be overcome by sinking the feature into the ground and again providing some form of ramp.

A JETTY built out over the water makes a useful platform for pond-dipping

NATIVE FLOWERING PLANTS attract pollinating insects while clumps of reeds and rushes provide cover for shy mammals

NATIVE MARGINAL PLANTS in soil blur the division between water and dry land, creating a wetland habitat

NATIVE TREES AND SHRUBS increase the habitat and enclose the pond. Such waterside plants may include goat willow (*Salix caprea*), white willow (*S. alba*), osier (*S. viminalis*) and guelder rose (*Viburnum opulus*)

SUITABLE NATIVE PLANTS

Oxygenating plants Curled pondweed (*Potamogeton crispus*), water crowfoot (*Ranunculus aquaticus*)

Floating-leaved plants Frogbit (*Hydrocharis morsus-ranae*), water fringe (*Nymphoides peltata*) and, for large ponds only, white water lily (*Nymphaea alba*)

Marginal plants Sweet flag (*Acorus calamus*), flowering rush (*Butomus umbellatus*), marsh marigold (*Caltha palustris*), yellow flag (*Iris pseudacorus*), bog bean (*Menyanthes trifoliata*), brooklime (*Veronica beccabunga*)

Moisture-loving plants Meadowsweet (*Filipendula ulmaria*), marsh St John's wort (*Hypericum elodes*), purple loosestrife (*Lythrum salicaria*), globe flower (*Trollius europaeus*)

Planting, stocking and maintenance

Above: **Native marginal plants such as flag iris (*Iris pseudacorus*) are beautiful as well as beneficial to wildlife**

Useful tips

- Acquiring some water, silt and plants from a donor pond will bring in small creatures, eggs and larvae and get the pond off to a flying start

- Leave some piles of stones or logs near the pond to provide shade, shelter and hibernation sites for amphibians

- If you want to keep fish as well, consider installing a separate pond

PLANTING

The richest pond habitat will be achieved by planting species native to your country or region. This is because the wildlife you want to attract has adapted itself to these plants, which may not be the case with more exotic species. Local ponds and nature reserves will provide you with inspiration and ideas on the type of plants suitable for your location. Although your choice of species is more limited, many natives are very attractive and being simpler in form and flower they look right in the wildlife pond setting. Plants from damp meadow habitats such as meadowsweet (*Filipendula ulmaria*) and purple loosestrife (*Lythrum salicaria*) can be introduced into the moist soil at the water's edge or into an adjacent wetland or bog garden. Garden plants as well as native trees and shrubs can be used as a backdrop to the pond, but avoid brightly coloured flowers and coloured or variegated leaves as they will look too ornamental. Aim for a quiet harmony more in keeping with the idea of a natural pond.

STOCKING

It is quite amazing how even the smallest area of water will miraculously attract life, and this is part of the fascination of a wildlife pond. The first arrivals will be insects such as pond-skaters and water boatmen as these are able to fly to new ponds. Damselflies and dragonflies will also find their way, using ponds as breeding sites and laying their eggs on

Left: **Water boatmen (*Corixa punctata*) will arrive of their own accord and will move through the water by using their legs as oars**

the stems of marginal plants. They spend much of their adult life darting across the water eating midges and small flies.

Certain creatures are useful in your pond as they eat algae and pond debris, helping to keep the water clear. The ramshorn snail is most commonly introduced for this purpose, along with freshwater mussels for larger ponds. The great pond snail is spectacular, but beware – it can be a bit too voracious in its eating habits.

Above: **Except during the mating season, smooth newts (*Triturus vulgaris*) are secretive and live mainly underwater**

Frogs, toads and newts are also beneficial pond creatures, spending much of their time in moist areas of the garden eating slugs and insects. They breed in the pond, laying their spawn in shallow water, or, in the case of newts, wrapping their eggs in submerged leaves. Adult amphibians will arrive at your pond of their own accord, although you can introduce spawn collected from an overpopulated pond (never from the wild). Frogs and toads take several years to reach maturity, so to establish a long-term population you need to add new

Above: Azure damselflies (*Coenagrion puella*) are the most beautiful of pond insects with their dazzling colours

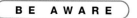

spawn for a couple of years in succession. They are migratory creatures that return to their home pond for breeding. In a well-established pond that has developed a natural balance there is no need to feed amphibians.

Ornamental (exotic) fish are not really compatible with the concept of a wildlife pond and do not mix with the native pond-life you want to encourage. Goldfish are carnivorous and will eat dragonfly larvae, frogspawn and tadpoles. Fish can also disturb pond sediment and eat beneficial water fleas which help keep algae under control. This affects the water quality and hence its ability to support life. If you really want fish in your wildlife pond, opt for suitably small native species such as sticklebacks or possibly tench. However, even sticklebacks will eat frogspawn so you will need to protect this in spring.

MAINTENANCE

Wildlife ponds should never be treated with chemicals and algicides to clear up an algae problem. This would upset the natural balance that has developed and

Right: A wildlife pond should be secluded and peaceful, so add a bench where you can enjoy the tranquillity of the scene

anyway would not be a long-term solution. Remove blanket weed by hand and leave it on the side of the pond overnight to allow creatures to crawl back into the water. It can then be put on the compost heap. Try to remove excessive plant growth at a time when disturbance to the wildlife is minimal; early autumn is preferable as the breeding season is over and hibernation is yet to start. The clearance of the dead and dying leaves of marginal plants is also an important task, but in a wildlife pond you should leave a fair amount of dead seed heads and tall stems uncut. These act as overwintering sites for invertebrates and emergence sites for spring insects such as dragonfly larvae that crawl up the stems prior to their final moult. Dense vegetation also provides valuable cover for amphibians as well as food and nesting material for birds and mammals, so do not be too eager to tidy everything up.

BE AWARE

● Some native plants, such as the great reedmace (*Typha latifolia*), are too vigorous for the garden pond

● Never collect amphibians or spawn from the wild to introduce into your pond – remember that you are trying to conserve wildlife, not remove it

Above: **Before the advent of pond liners concrete was the preferred method of containing water, as in this formal pond at the Majorelle Garden in Marrakech**

5 • Installation

H aving decided on the style of your pond or water feature and its size, shape and location within the garden, you are now in a position to start building. Unless you are lucky enough to have a natural pond or stream, you will need to adopt an artificial method of retaining the water. The traditional method of using clay to line and waterproof a hollow is only viable if a local supply is available in quantity and a large pond is being created. In most domestic situations there are really only three methods – concrete, preformed units or flexible liners. The one you choose will be based on a number of factors including the style and type of feature, your level of skill and enthusiasm, and your available time, labour and budget.

Concrete

Before the widespread use of plastics and rubber compounds, concrete was the preferred method of creating an artificial pond. It is a waterproof material that can be poured into a mould to make a pond or applied as a layer over a structure of concrete blocks. Making a concrete liner is heavy and labour-intensive work that requires a good level of skill to do properly, so it is generally advisable to employ a professional contractor. For this reason it is now the least popular method of pond construction, but it has its place: it is an ideal material where awkward angles and shapes need to be created and where

Left and *below:* **This large semi-circular pond has been created by installing a flexible pond liner that easily moulds itself to the contours of the marginal planting shelves. The pond sides and edgings have been constructed on top of the liner**

a liner (flexible or preformed) would be difficult to conceal. It is well suited to formal, especially split-level, ponds and to more contemporary treatments.

Preformed units

Preformed pond liners are made from rigid heavy-duty plastic or fibreglass and come in a wide range of shapes and sizes. They are popular because they have a fixed shape and a smooth internal surface. They are reasonably light to handle, relatively easy to install, and the outcome is predictable and instant. However, because they are quite small, shallow and steep-sided they can look too contrived in a naturalistic setting, and an informal planted edge is hard to achieve. The best use of preformed units is in formal designs where a geometric-shaped pond is required, either sunken or raised. In this case the artificial nature of the pond is not at odds with its surroundings as there is no pretence that the pond is a natural feature.

Flexible liners

Flexible liners are by far and away the most popular and cost-effective way of creating garden ponds. They are adaptable enough to line all types and styles of water feature, including bog gardens, and are especially suited to the informal shapes of wildlife and naturalistic ponds. Flexible liners are available in a variety of materials that vary in price according to their durability and ease of installation.

Polythene is the cheapest lining material but is also the least durable, having a life expectancy of 3–5 years. It is not particularly pliable and is prone to puncturing. It becomes brittle when exposed to sunlight but is useful for creating bog gardens as the liner is

Above: **A preformed liner has been used to create a circular sunken pond. The steep sides of the liner have been cleverly concealed with woven willow hurdles**

protected beneath soil. PVC liners come in a range of weights (thicknesses) and are a little more expensive, but the material is also more durable, lasting 10–15 years. It is slightly more flexible than polythene, though thicker gauges can be a little stiff and difficult to work.

The most durable material for flexible liners is butyl, an elastic rubber-based product that is usually sold with a lifetime guarantee. It is soft and easy to work, is highly resistant to puncturing and has an excellent resistance to ultraviolet light. Various grades are available, but the most usual is 0.75 mm (0.03 in). Butyl sheets can be welded together to line very large ponds or 'box welded' to line regular-shaped ponds.

Right: **The natural shape and shallow profile of this pond is made possible by a flexible liner. A layer of pebbles and cobbles makes an attractive base to the pond, protecting and disguising the liner**

Concrete ponds

Below: **This simple concrete trough is unashamedly modernist in form and finish. Its clean, contemporary lines are heightened in its setting amid naturalistic planting**

A concrete pond can be made from either poured concrete or precast blocks. Poured concrete requires a timber mould known as 'shuttering' to shape the pond, and will usually need reinforcement to prevent cracks resulting from ground movement. As this can be quite an involved process it is easier to use precast concrete blocks to make the pond structure, particularly where you want a regular-shaped or raised pond.

A CONCRETE POND

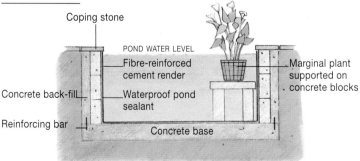

Coping stone

POND WATER LEVEL

Fibre-reinforced cement render

Concrete back-fill

Waterproof pond sealant

Reinforcing bar

Concrete base

Marginal plant supported on concrete blocks

Creating a concrete pond

To make a pond using concrete blocks, first mark the size and shape of your pond and excavate a hole to the required maximum depth, plus an extra 10–15 cm (4–6 in) for the pond base. Dampen the excavation and pour in a wet concrete mix over the compacted ground to form a raft or slab. Tamp it level with a length of timber and leave it to cure for two or three days.

When the foundation has cured, build the concrete block walls on top of it using mortar joints and a staggered bond as in a brick wall. To make the structure more stable, set steel reinforcing rods into the concrete foundation to connect the sides to the base and back-fill the excavation behind the blocks with poured concrete.

The pond can then be waterproofed with a special fibre-reinforced cement render and sealed with a purpose-made pond sealant. Sealing also ensures that no lime from the cement used in the concrete can find its way into the water, harming fish. Adding a dark pigment to the render, or using a dark-coloured sealant, will give the pond a greater sense of depth and make the water surface more reflective.

Alternatively, the rendered surface can be tiled, as in a swimming pool, allowing for plenty of creativity in terms of colour and pattern visible under

water. You need to make sure that the tiles and mosaics you select are suitable for external, underwater use.

Finally, the tops of the walls can be finished with a coping stone. Shelves for marginal plants can be made from extra concrete blocks.

A similar method can be used to construct a raised concrete pond. The concrete block walls must be thick enough to withstand the water pressure and strengthened with steel reinforcing bars. In a split-level pond, a purpose-made spillway can been fitted in order to allow water to spill from one pond to the other.

Left: Concrete is an ideal material to use in difficult situations such as this series of interconnected circular ponds. The external walls have been faced with stone and topped with specially cut coping stones

Above: A concrete surface allows for the application of decorative tiles, such as these mosaics on the base of a shallow pond

Above: Here stainless steel spillways have been designed to fit seamlessly into the concrete structure of the pond

A SPLIT-LEVEL CONCRETE POND WITH SPILLWAY

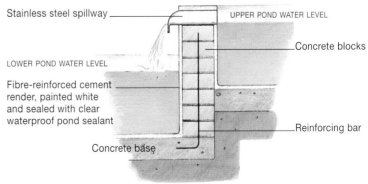

Stainless steel spillway

UPPER POND WATER LEVEL

Concrete blocks

LOWER POND WATER LEVEL

Fibre-reinforced cement render, painted white and sealed with clear waterproof pond sealant

Reinforcing bar

Concrete base

Preformed-liner ponds

You can make a pond from a preformed liner or unit by simply digging a hole in the ground to the correct size and shape for the liner and ensuring that it is perfectly level. This type of liner installation is consequently ideal for those with modest DIY skills, especially when the pond is relatively small and regularly shaped. Preformed liners and units can be used to create raised or semi-raised ponds, but in this case it is best to choose a small unit with only one depth, as larger, irregularly shaped ones with different depth zones are difficult to support properly. Once filled the unit will be very heavy and if it is not fully supported any ground settlement could cause it to fracture.

Above: **These small preformed units have been installed with fountain jets and set at regular intervals within a low box hedge**

EDGING STONES

If paving slabs or stone are used to edge the pond you must provide sufficient support to bear their weight. This can be achieved by digging a 15 cm (6 in) trench where the edging is to go and filling it with aggregate, ensuring that some is placed under the pond lip. The slabs or stones can then be mortared into place.

Top and above: **This circular preformed pond unit makes an ideal liner for a raised pond. Only the wall foundations need digging as the liner sits on ground level. The coping stones match the walling and overhang the pond to disguise the liner**

A PREFORMED-LINER POND

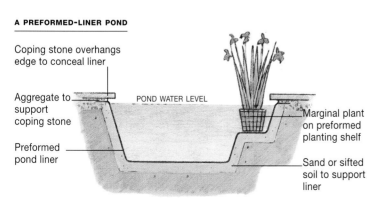

Coping stone overhangs edge to conceal liner

Aggregate to support coping stone

POND WATER LEVEL

Preformed pond liner

Marginal plant on preformed planting shelf

Sand or sifted soil to support liner

Above: **This trough made from fibreglass looks convincingly like natural stone, and makes an attractive feature in its own right**

INSTALLING A PREFORMED-LINER POND

1 Place the preformed pond unit in position and carefully mark its outline on the ground with pegs and string. Remove the unit, leaving the ground ready for excavation.

2 It is important that the excavation matches the profile of the unit. To establish the depth of excavation required for the planting shelves, measure the unit from the rim to the planting shelf.

3 Begin to excavate the hole by digging at a distance of 15–20 cm (6–8 in) outside the string line. This allows for plenty of space around the installed pond unit for later back-filling.

4 Remove all stones and sharp objects from within the excavation and firm and level the bottom of the hole, paying particular attention to the edges where the marginal shelves will rest.

5 Check the depth of the excavation before marking the position of the deep zone within the hole. Measure the depth of the deep zone, plus an extra 5 cm (2 in), and dig it out.

6 Smooth the sides of the excavation, again removing any stones, and spread a 5 cm (2 in) protective layer of sand on the base and sides of the hole before lowering the unit into position.

7 Press the unit gently into place until it is level, adjusting the contours of the excavation if necessary. Partially fill the pond with water to settle it into place and make it more stable.

8 Back-fill around the pond with sifted soil or sand, tamping it down as you go. Keep checking the level as you back-fill, tamp down and fill the pond with water, 10 cm (4 in) at a time.

9 Leave the pond to settle into position in the excavation for a few days before installing the edging. A simple timber surround can made from boards secured to short supporting posts.

10 The finished pond has been given a slightly tropical setting by fixing a reed panel to the boundary fence and planting a range of colourful and bold-leaved plants complemented with bamboos and grasses.

11 With ponds created from steep-sided preformed units it is important to place a suitable stone or ramp on the planting shelf to allow easy access and exit for pond creatures.

LINER SIZE

To calculate the length of liner required, take the maximum length of the pond and add twice the depth. Repeat for the width. Add 45 cm (18 in) to both dimensions to allow for overlapping on the rim of the pond.

Flexible-liner ponds

At its simplest, making a pond with a flexible liner involves excavating a hole, placing the liner into the hole and filling it with water. Depending upon your skills and enthusiasm, this basic approach can be extended to create all manner of ponds with relative ease, be they informal, formal, sunken or raised. A flexible liner will mould itself to whatever pond you choose to create, giving you complete control over its size, shape and profile. This frees you from the restrictions that are imposed by a preformed pond liner, though you will have to calculate the amount of liner required (see box, left) and take precautions to protect the liner fabric from punctures.

PROTECTING THE LINER

Underlay material made of woven fabric is used in conjunction with flexible liners to provide protection against roots and stones. It is available in wide rolls, making it an easy job to cover the pond base. The fabric can also be used on top of the liner where structures and edgings are to be built in the pond. Sand or old carpet can be used as an alternative.

Below and right: **Even in formal ponds, flexible liners are the best way of containing the water. Rendered concrete blocks form the walls and are built within the liner. A layer of concrete on the bottom protects the liner from sunlight and puncture**

A FLEXIBLE-LINER POND

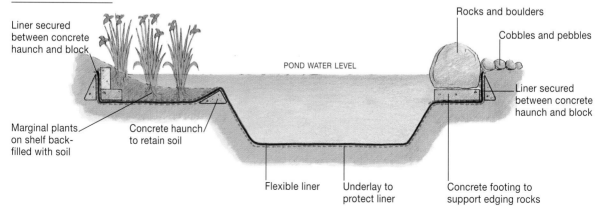

Liner secured between concrete haunch and block

Rocks and boulders

Cobbles and pebbles

POND WATER LEVEL

Liner secured between concrete haunch and block

Marginal plants on shelf back-filled with soil

Concrete haunch to retain soil

Flexible liner

Underlay to protect liner

Concrete footing to support edging rocks

INSTALLING A FLEXIBLE-LINER POND

1 For an informal pond, transfer your design onto the ground using a hosepipe. Check the size and shape from a variety of viewpoints and when you are satisfied, mark the line with sand.

2 To set the level of the finished pond edge, drive a datum peg into the ground on the sand line. Using a spirit level, place further pegs around the pond outline at the same level.

3 Begin to dig the hole for the pond within the outline you have marked (for a large pond you might consider hiring an excavator). Try to use the excavated soil elsewhere in the garden.

4 Continue to excavate until you have achieved the profile you want, with marginal shelves and deeper zones where appropriate. Remember to include a shelf for the pond edging.

5 Remove any stones and sharp objects from the bottom and sides of the excavation and spread out a protective underlay material, pressing it firmly into the contours of the pond.

6 Place the liner over the hole, making sure you have a generous overlap on all sides. Gently smooth it into place, without pulling it taut, and fold in any creases and pleats as neatly as you can.

7 Begin to install the pond edge by laying further protective underlay on top of the liner and constructing a concrete footing around the rim to accept and support the chosen edging material.

8 For a natural rock-edged pond, mortar any larger rocks in position over the footings. Place smaller cobbles and pebbles around them to create a beach edge and disguise the liner.

9 Once the edges have been securely installed, the pond can be carefully filled with water. Any surplus liner beyond the edges can then be trimmed off flush with the ground using a sharp knife.

10 A variety of edge treatments have been chosen for this pond and a stone island has been included, supported on a pier built off the liner. After the water has settled the pond and surrounds are ready to plant.

11 The oriental-style pond has been given a small promontory to represent a rocky coastline. This provides a base for a traditional stone lantern to act as a focal point and reflect in the water.

Edging the pond

The key to success with any pond or water feature lies in hiding the mechanics of its construction, allowing the feature to be enjoyed without the magic being betrayed by visible liners, cables and pipes. The detailing of the pond edge is most important in this respect. As well as giving the pond its character, the edging secures and protects the structure of the pond lining so that no damage or movement can occur.

Concrete ponds

As concrete ponds tend to be formal in style and placement, masonry materials such as brick, stone or concrete are the best choice for the edging. To create a unified design, fit the edge at the same time as you build the pond and lay the surrounding paving.

Preformed-liner ponds

Most materials can be used to edge preformed ponds as long as they project over the edge to hide the liner. This makes materials of larger size such as paving stones an ideal choice, as well as

Above: **In shallow ponds it is sensible to protect the liner from ultra-violet light. Here the base has been covered with a decorative layer of stones**

timber boards and decking. The only way to achieve a soft edge and hide the liner is to plant evergreen groundcovers close to the edge, allowing them to flop over the sides. The steep sides of preformed-liner ponds are difficult to conceal and inevitably the liner becomes exposed when the water level drops, so you must keep the pond topped up.

Flexible-liner ponds

One of the many advantages of flexible liners is that they allow for a great variety of edging treatments. Those described on the following pages can be modified to suit any situation. The principle behind each one is to conceal the liner and protect it from sharp materials and deterioration by exposure to ultra-violet light. In all cases the liner is protected with an underlay material (shown with a dotted line). Many of the details could be adapted for concrete ponds. Select the edging material and construction method to suit the style of your pond and your level of skill.

Left: **Here a number of edging materials have been combined, from soft plants and pebble beaches to brick and decking**

Planted edges

Soft, planted edges are easy to create and suit informal and wildlife ponds that are not subject to much wear and tear. Soil is used to cover the liner and provide the medium into which marginal and moisture-loving plants can root, blurring the pond edge. A large stone can be mortared to the front edge of the marginal planting shelf to stop the soil slipping to the bottom of the pond.

Beach edges

A gently shelving beach is an appropriate edge for informal and wildlife ponds. The cobbles can simply be laid, or mortared in place, on the liner over a shallow profile (see pages 64–5), or the edge of the pond can be strengthened with concrete to withstand the weight of people. A large stone mortared on the front edge of the beach will prevent the cobbles slipping to the bottom of the pond. Rounded cobbles and pebbles associate better with water and a variety of sizes will create a more natural effect.

Turf edges

A natural grass edge can be achieved by simply laying turf over soil on the liner beyond the water's edge. This is not particularly hard-wearing and a crisper, more secure edge can be created by laying turf on top of perforated concrete blocks set on concrete footings. The holes in the blocks are filled with soil to allow the turf to root and the sides are painted black to make them less visible. Perforated engineering bricks, which are impermeable to frost, can also be used.

A PLANTED EDGE

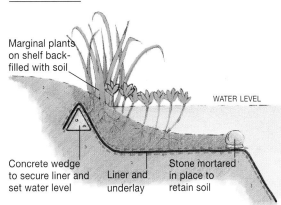

Marginal plants on shelf back-filled with soil

WATER LEVEL

Concrete wedge to secure liner and set water level

Liner and underlay

Stone mortared in place to retain soil

A BEACH EDGE

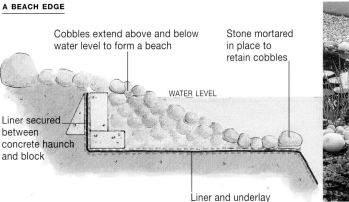

Cobbles extend above and below water level to form a beach

Stone mortared in place to retain cobbles

WATER LEVEL

Liner secured between concrete haunch and block

Liner and underlay

A TURF EDGE

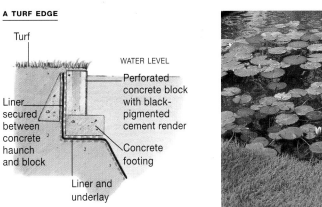

Turf

WATER LEVEL

Liner secured between concrete haunch and block

Perforated concrete block with black-pigmented cement render

Concrete footing

Liner and underlay

Natural rock edges

An edge of rounded boulders or natural stone can enhance the appearance of an informal pond. Set them on concrete footings with their bases below water level. A natural look can be created by varying the sizes and placing some further into the water as well as in the ground beyond the pond to link it to the surroundings. Small rocks can look too busy and temporary so it is worth hiring lifting equipment if necessary to place larger boulders.

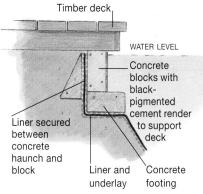

A NATURAL ROCK EDGE

Rocks and boulders

WATER LEVEL

Concrete footing to support edging rocks

Liner secured between concrete haunch and block

Liner and underlay

Timber edges

Timber suits both formal and informal ponds and a wide range of edgings can be made, from vertical log sections to horizontally laid planks. Even softwood can now have a long lifespan if treated with preservatives, although any timber treatments in contact with the pond water must be safe for aquatic life.

Short timber stakes make an excellent pond edge where a clearly defined but still informal treatment is required. Their small diameter means that curving shapes can easily be accommodated. The stakes are set vertically in a concrete footing, into which a dark pigment can be added to make it less visible below water.

A timber deck can be built adjacent to the pond with sufficient overhang to hide the liner and give a sense of the water disappearing beneath. The deck is supported on black-painted concrete blocks set on concrete footings. Decks can be extended further into the pond by cantilevering out from the edge or by building a support off the liner (see pages 88–9).

A TIMBER STAKE EDGE

Timber stake

WATER LEVEL

Liner secured between concrete haunch and block

Concrete footing

Liner and underlay

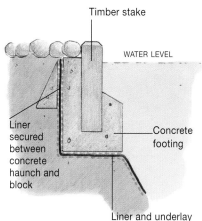

A TIMBER DECK EDGE

Timber deck

WATER LEVEL

Concrete blocks with black-pigmented cement render to support deck

Liner secured between concrete haunch and block

Liner and underlay

Concrete footing

Paved edges

Paving units in the form of slabs, tiles, bricks and blocks are ideal materials to edge a formal pond and should be chosen to match or complement surrounding surfaces. A contrasting material will give a clearly defined edge. The edge is supported on a low wall built on a concrete footing beneath the liner, which is pulled up vertically behind the wall and secured with concrete. Paved edges must be laid accurately, as an uneven surface will be obvious adjacent to a horizontal plane of water.

Engineering and paving bricks (pavers) are ideal for pond edgings, being hard and impermeable to frost. They should be laid side to side rather than end to end to create a more secure and pleasing edge. Brick contrasts well with surrounding surface materials and provides a crisp, neat division between paving and pond.

Stone can be used in a variety of ways for edging, from preformed slabs, blocks and setts to specially cut sections to fit a particular design. The stone edge can be a continuation of the paving surrounding the pond or a contrasting strip. Concrete slabs and terracotta tiles can be used in the same way.

Metal edges

A metal edge will give a formal pond a contemporary appearance. It can be achieved by bending a length of soft sheet metal such as copper over a concrete block wall, built as for paved edges, and secured with galvanized screws. A harder metal such as stainless steel would need to be prefabricated.

A PAVED EDGE: STONE

Stone slab

WATER LEVEL

Concrete blocks with black-pigmented cement render

Liner secured between concrete back-fill and blocks

Concrete footing

Liner and underlay

A PAVED EDGE: BRICK

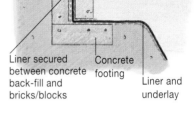

Brick on edge (with chamfer)

WATER LEVEL

Brick

Concrete block

Liner secured between concrete back-fill and bricks/blocks

Concrete footing

Liner and underlay

A METAL EDGE

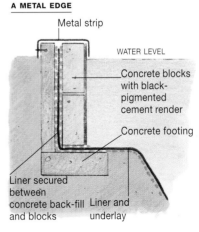

Metal strip

WATER LEVEL

Concrete blocks with black-pigmented cement render

Concrete footing

Liner secured between concrete back-fill and blocks

Liner and underlay

Raised ponds

Edging the pond and disguising the liner in a raised feature requires a little more thought but can easily be achieved with a flexible liner. The method will vary according to the design of the pond and the materials used in its construction, but the walls must be sufficiently strong to withstand the pressure of the water. They will need to be at least 23 cm (9 in) thick and wider still in areas where winter weather is particularly severe.

Masonry walls Brick and stone are ideal materials for creating raised ponds, the liner being hidden within the construction so that it is not visible from either side. It is sandwiched between the outer wall of the pond and an inner one built on the liner over a concrete footing. The liner is cut flush with the top of the walls and a coping stone or brick is mortared in place to protect the wall and hide the construction. Because the pond walls are thick the coping can be made wide enough to sit on.

A RAISED POND

Coping stone
Bricks
Liner secured between outer brick and inner block walls
Concrete footing
WATER LEVEL
Concrete blocks
Liner and underlay

Above: Wide coping stones provide a neat and secure finish to the walls of this raised pond

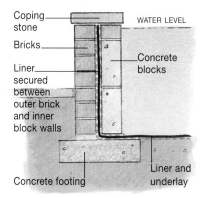

A RAISED STONE POND

Stone slab coping
Outer stone block wall
WATER LEVEL
Inner stone block wall
Concrete footing
Concrete footing
Liner and underlay

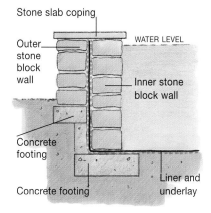

A RAISED BRICK POND

Double row brick on edge coping
Outer brick wall
Concrete fill
WATER LEVEL
Inner concrete block wall
Concrete footing
Concrete footing
Liner and underlay

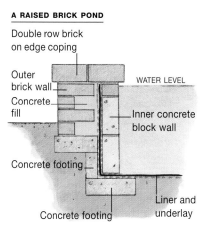

Above: The small unit size of brick makes this an ideal material for creating a circular pond

Timber walls A raised pond can be built using railway sleepers stacked on top of each other and held together with steel bars angled into concrete footings. The pond liner is brought up on the inside of the timbers and behind a timber fascia board and is secured with stainless steel (rustproof) screws set at a distance of about 5 cm (2 in) below the top of the highest railway sleeper. Because the screws puncture the pond liner they effectively set the maximum water level.

Brimming ponds

Raising the water to the level of the surrounding edging can create an attractive brimming effect. To achieve this in a sunken pond, the liner should be brought up behind the edging units as well as the pond walls before being trimmed off flush with the surface. In a raised pond the coping units must have a double width in order that the liner can be brought up between the units as well as the walls. Different materials will suggest slightly different methods of construction.

A RAISED TIMBER POND

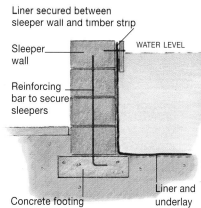

Liner secured between sleeper wall and timber strip

WATER LEVEL

Sleeper wall

Reinforcing bar to secure sleepers

Concrete footing

Liner and underlay

Above: **Water flows between stone setts to create an unusual edge to this brimming pond**

A BRIMMING POND WITH A BRICK EDGE

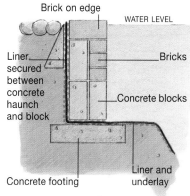

Brick on edge

WATER LEVEL

Liner secured between concrete haunch and block

Bricks

Concrete blocks

Concrete footing

Liner and underlay

A BRIMMING POND WITH A STONE EDGE

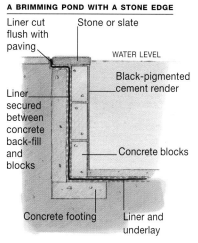

Liner cut flush with paving

Stone or slate

WATER LEVEL

Black-pigmented cement render

Liner secured between concrete back-fill and blocks

Concrete blocks

Concrete footing

Liner and underlay

Above: **This pebble-covered stream is essentially a sloping waterfall or 'rapid' that will run dry when the pump is turned off**

Streams, rills and waterfalls

If you do not have a natural watercourse running through your garden but want to include a moving water feature you will need to create it artificially. A slight level change across your plot will allow you to move water from higher to lower ground and create either a natural-looking stream or a more formal rill. Waterfalls will be created where level changes occur along the length of both types of watercourse.

Streams and rills are self-contained features where the water is circulated by an electric pump from a receiving pond or reservoir via a delivery pipe to the source of the feature, returning to the pond under the force of gravity.

Streams and waterfalls

A stream should look natural, so its course should not be too complicated or winding as this will seem artificial and contrived. The contours of the garden will dictate the line to a certain extent, although spoil from the stream or pond excavation can be used to develop the contours around the feature and make it appear more natural and settled.

It is possible to construct a stream on sloping ground without any waterfalls,

Below: **In this classic rill water bubbles up in a header pool before making its way down a water staircase to a lower canal and on to its destination of a circular formal pond**

Above: **A 'flow-form' is a preformed waterfall unit designed to aerate water and keep it clear and healthy for fish and other pondlife**

although this approach can cause problems. Where the slope is too steep the water will quickly run to the bottom and the pump will have a hard time keeping up with the speed of the flow; if the pump is turned off at any time the stream will continue to flow until the water has collected at the bottom, leaving the stream itself empty.

The best plan is to design a stream with a few interruptions in the watercourse, effectively resulting in a series of interconnected small pools. The change in level between these pools can be barely perceptible, the advantage being that the water will remain in place even when the pump is not running. Increasing the level change between the pools will result in waterfalls and by varying the heights of falls along the course a more natural effect can be achieved.

The pond or reservoir at the destination of the stream needs to be big enough to prime the system without causing a noticeable drop of water level. The pump will remove water from this pond in order to start the stream running and the level of water in each part of the feature has to rise sufficiently high to allow it to spill over into the next. Therefore the volume of water in the receiving pond must be sufficient for this to happen without it emptying. If the receiver pond were topped up to make up for a drop in water level the stream would continue to flow even after the pump has been switched off, causing the receiving pond to overflow, so it is important to get this right.

The source of the stream is an important detail, especially if you want to create the illusion of water issuing from a natural origin. The water outlet served by the delivery pipe can be disguised with rockwork or plants, or a hidden pool or reservoir can be created, allowing the recirculating water to spill into the stream more gently. This 'header pool' is filled from the delivery pipe until it spills over into the stream, thus avoiding the unnatural appearance of a spout of water. Provided the pipe enters above water level or is fitted with a non-return valve, water will not siphon back to the receiving pond.

Right: The source of this pebble-covered stream is a ceramic spill pan on the edge of a deck – a feature in its own right

Design focus

• A long stream can be fitted with a second outlet further downstream to increase the flow rate. Gate valves on the delivery pipes will allow the rates to be balanced to create the desired effect

• A successful waterfall depends on positioning stone and rock to create a natural appearance. Study waterfalls in nature and use stone that is local to your region

Installing a stream

The construction of a meandering stream is similar to that of informal ponds, and the versatility of flexible liners makes them the ideal choice. It may be possible to construct a relatively straight stream with just a few, or very small, falls using a single piece of liner, but it is generally necessary to employ a number of overlapping pieces to create a series of interconnected self-contained pools. The rockwork for each pool in the stream is contained within independent butyl liner 'bags'.

Each pool needs a spillway stone, flanked by taller stones, over which the water flows when the system is switched on. The changes in level between each pool in the stream must be appropriate to the slope of the ground and the effect you are after.

The stream should be built from the lower end, working upwards, with each pool lined as for a flexible liner pond (see pages 74–5). All the stones should be securely mortared in place over concrete footings on top of the liner, which is protected with underlay. The liner for each pool must overlap with, or be butted to, the liner from the pool below to prevent leaks. The liners are sandwiched behind the spillway stone

Above: **In this newly installed stream two water outlets have been fitted, one at the head of the feature and a second to increase the flow rate further downstream**

Top and above: **A watertight joint between sections of stream can be achieved by butting the liners together and sandwiching them behind the spillway stone. The liners are protected with underlay and the join is sealed and disguised with mortar**

A ROCK-EDGED STREAM

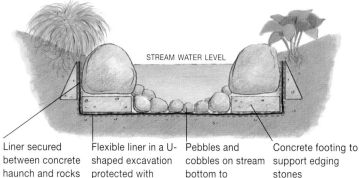

STREAM WATER LEVEL

Liner secured between concrete haunch and rocks

Flexible liner in a U-shaped excavation protected with underlay

Pebbles and cobbles on stream bottom to disguise liner

Concrete footing to support edging stones

A PROFILE OF A STREAM WITH WATERFALLS

A stream is a series of pools contained within independent, overlapping butyl liners.

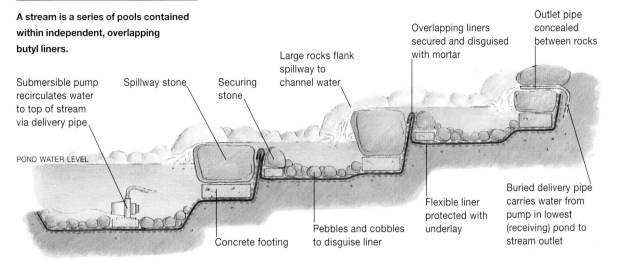

Submersible pump recirculates water to top of stream via delivery pipe

Spillway stone

Securing stone

Large rocks flank spillway to channel water

Overlapping liners secured and disguised with mortar

Outlet pipe concealed between rocks

POND WATER LEVEL

Concrete footing

Pebbles and cobbles to disguise liner

Flexible liner protected with underlay

Buried delivery pipe carries water from pump in lowest (receiving) pond to stream outlet

by a further securing stone. Mortar is used between the stones, concealing the liners and waterproofing the joint completely. Throwing handfuls of earth onto the wet mortar will disguise it, making it blend with the rock.

A submersible pump is positioned in the lowest pond (or in a separate pump chamber linked to the pond) and recirculates the water via a buried delivery pipe to the source of the stream (see profile above).

Waterfalls and spillways

The spillway stone over which the water flows to create a waterfall should be chosen carefully for the effect you want. A stone with a slight overhang will cast water away from the rock face, creating a smooth sheet. One with a backward slope will allow water to flow down the rock-face, tracing its rough outline. A narrow spillway will accelerate the flow and create a thin ribbon of water, while a wide spillway will slow it down and create a broad curtain of water. Further variations to the fall are possible by placing rocks in its path and forming breaks and patterns in the falling water.

Right: Here a wide, jagged-edged spillway stone projects out beyond the rock-face, causing the sheet of water to split into a series of ribbons

Left: This spillway stone channels water over onto a 'carp' stone which divides the flow, creating a finer effect and gentler sound as it hits the water in the pool below

see also	page
• Flexible-liner ponds	74
• Edging the pond	76
• Electricity in the garden	90
• Planted streams	102

Above: **This narrow canal draws the eye along its length, suggesting movement**

Design focus

• Sloping the edges of a rill or canal to follow the fall of the land will look wrong. It is far better to install some waterfalls to step rather than slope the feature

• A rill can be constructed from concrete but any ground movement along its length could cause the concrete to crack and leak. Flexible liners are a much better option

• A successful rill design will be one that uses materials to match or complement those used in the rest of the garden

Rills, canals and spillways

Rills and canals can simply be regarded as man-made streams, a geometric version of a natural watercourse. It is not strictly necessary for water to run from one end to the other as their linear nature in itself suggests movement, but where water flow is required it can be induced by means of a rill spilling water into a pond set at a slightly lower

level. A pump is used to recirculate the water back to the outlet or source of the rill.

The source needs careful thought, as it must be in keeping with the formal nature of the feature. The outlet could enter a header pool and then simply spill over into the rill; it could enter the rill from a hidden pool through an opening or spout; or it could enter from a fountain feature. Where there is a slope along the length of the rill a series of waterfalls can be a most effective feature. In this case the falls should be designed as a clearly man-made feature, a water step rather than a naturalistic fall.

Left and below: **Rendered concrete blocks form the walls of this rill and water staircase, with the whole structure contained within a flexible liner. The rill and water staircase has been edged and lined with a smooth slate, and for continuity the slate continues across to edge and surface the steps**

Installing a rill

Rills and canals are constructed in the same way as streams by using a flexible liner as a waterproof bag within which the rill is constructed. The liner can then be completely hidden by the material used to face the construction. This is particularly important in a rill, where the effect should be one of crispness and formality. Waterfalls and staircases within the rill also need to be formal in character, allowing the water either to hug the surface of the spillway for a gentle effect or to flow over an overhanging spillway to create a smooth curtain of water. Flow rates are perhaps even more critical for a rill than for an informal stream (see box, page 84).

Above and right: The source of a rill can be either a decorative feature such as this granite bowl or concealed in a 'header pool' from where the water emerges over a spillway

A SHALLOW RILL

Water skims along the surface of this perfectly level rill by means of the constant flow from the source to a receiving pond at a lower level. Because the rill is shallow the internal surfaces are clearly visible and the base stone has been chosen to match the edging stones.

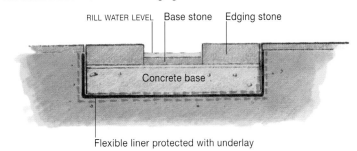

A DEEP RILL

Water is held in a series of independent pools along this rill. As it flows from the source the water level in each pool rises and flows into the pool below. The internal surface is coloured black to give a greater sense of depth.

Top and above: Formal falls can be designed so that the water either hugs the surface to create a gentle trickling sound, here in a shallow rill, or projects out in a curtain effect to make a louder, splashing sound, as in the deeper rill

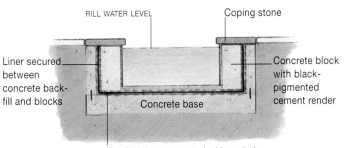

Above: **A timber bridge supported on timber posts spans a narrow stream**

Above: **This timber deck is supported on steel joists over a concrete foundation**

FOUNDATIONS

Concrete footings at least 15 cm (6 in) deep are needed to spread the weight of structures. Footings should be built on top of the liner and the liner protected with underlay. On soft ground it may be necessary to stabilize the areas where the structures are to be built with a layer of concrete or compacted hardcore beneath the liner. In concrete ponds there is usually no need for footings.

Structures in the pond

A bridge will allow you to cross over your pond or stream, and a deck or jetty will give you closer access to the water. Unless the structure is cantilevered off the pond edge or is long enough to bridge the water in a single span it will need to be built off the liner at the base of the pond at the same time that the pond is installed. This is also true of any islands or stepping stones you may wish to include. As with any surfaces adjacent to water, safety is an important issue and all structures must be firm and non-slip.

Bridges, decks and jetties

A bridge should be located at the most natural point to cross the water. It should complement the look and character of the pond and be designed to fit its intended purpose. A simple footbridge need only be wide enough to be safe, whereas a bridge required to carry lawnmowers and wheelbarrows needs to be more substantial. Jetties and decks are effectively open-ended bridges that project out over the water.

Handrails should be considered if a bridge, deck or jetty is at all high or if

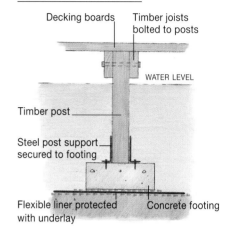

A BRIDGE OR JETTY SUPPORT

Decking boards — Timber joists bolted to posts

WATER LEVEL

Timber post _____

Steel post support secured to footing

Flexible liner protected with underlay — Concrete footing

safety is an issue. They can be attractive features and provided they are solid and secure they can be leant upon so that you can gaze into the water. Consider filling in the sides with vertical timber slats or unobtrusive wire netting where young children are present.

Timber structures should be made according to good carpentry practice with boards, joists and supporting members, correctly jointed and secured with galvanized (rust-proof) fixings. The 'dry' ends of the structure must be securely supported on appropriate foundations. Depending upon the construction method used, a bridge can span up to 2.4m (8ft) without a central support but for a structure longer than this, or where materials dictate, supporting piers will be required in the water.

Left: **The rectangular granite slabs used to create this oriental-style bridge are supported on granite boulders secured on the liner on the bottom of the pond**

Stepping stones

Stepping stones need to be large enough to be safe and spaced close enough to allow easy passage. They should be at least 40 cm (16 in) square or diameter, although the material from which they are made will largely determine their size and shape. Their placement within the pond needs to complement the design of the whole water feature.

Stepping stones must be secure and solid. In shallow water they can be placed directly on the liner and secured in position with mortar. In deeper water each stone must be placed on a pier built from concrete blocks or bricks on top of the liner. The stepping stone is then secured to the top of the pier.

Islands

Generally speaking a pond needs to be quite large to incorporate an island, although single boulders in a small pond look effective. If the island is intended as a wildlife retreat it must be at least 1.2 m (4 ft) wide to accommodate the required planting cover and far enough from the pond edges to deter predators. It can be built on top of the liner using rocks or sandbags and the resulting structure back-filled with heavy (clay-based) topsoil in readiness for planting.

A STEPPING STONE

Stepping stone securely fixed to pier

Overhang to create impression of 'floating' stepping stones

WATER LEVEL

Brick pier

Black-pigmented cement render

Concrete footing

Flexible liner protected with underlay

Above: Here square-edged stepping stones built off the liner reflect the regularity of the surrounding surfaces and edgings

Above: These rocks have been carefully grouped and supported on a wide concrete footing built off the liner

Above: A rock island can be made by raising a boulder to the correct level on a pier

Far left and left: This foaming boulder is essentially an island set into the pond. It is supported on both sides by blocks, allowing the delivery pipe for the fountain to be fed through a drilled hole in the centre of the stone

89

Electricity in the garden

Useful tips

• Select a pump slightly larger than that required as flow rates can always be adjusted down

• Never let a submersible pump run dry because the motor will be damaged

• Locate the pump on a block to raise it above debris on the pond bottom

With the number of products now available, adding the excitement of moving water and lighting to your garden has never been easier and more cost-effective. Electrical products can either be mains or low voltage. Low voltage is adequate for most lighting applications and for small pumps but mains will be required for more powerful pumps and will allow you more choice of fittings. Low-voltage systems use a transformer (usually located indoors near to the mains supply) to reduce the voltage, making the supply safe in the event of a short circuit or damaged cable. Mains supply is safe provided that cables are correctly installed. Cabling must be armoured or buried at least 45 cm (18 in) deep in a trench within a protective conduit.

All sockets and connectors must be designed for outdoor use and fitted by a qualified electrician conforming to local regulations. Ensure that the correct fuse rating is used for your equipment.

Pumps

Pumps are used to recirculate water. An electric motor draws water through a filter and pushes it out through a pipe attached to an outlet such as a fountain. A flow adjuster is usually fitted to the pump, allowing a degree of control over the output. Pumps are either 'surface' (housed above water) or 'submersible' (underwater). Surface pumps need a dry, well-ventilated housing and are noisy and more expensive to run. Unless a particularly powerful pump is required, for a large cascade for example, submersible pumps are the best option.

The choice of pump for your pond or water feature is wide and is dictated by its intended use. Suppliers will help with the specific choice but will need to know what feature the pump is for, what volume of water you want to move and at what rate, and whether it will run continuously.

If the pump is to supply a waterfall you need to know the distance from the surface of the pond to the top of the fall. This is known as the 'head' of water. The higher the head, the greater the power of the pump required. You will also need to know the width of the waterfall (see page 84).

Filters

Filters are used to help establish and maintain a healthy water quality for fish (see pages 122–3). Where no fish are present, or where a pond is only lightly stocked, a well-planned planting scheme will act as a biological filter and will be perfectly adequate to maintain a well-balanced and healthy water quality (see Chapter 6).

A SUBMERSIBLE PUMP

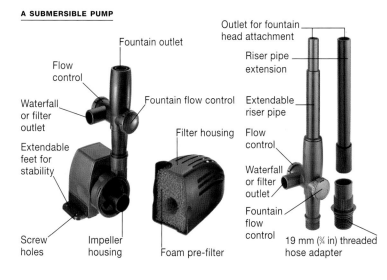

Fountain outlet

Flow control

Waterfall or filter outlet

Extendable feet for stability

Screw holes

Impeller housing

Fountain flow control

Filter housing

Foam pre-filter

Outlet for fountain head attachment

Riser pipe extension

Extendable riser pipe

Flow control

Waterfall or filter outlet

Fountain flow control

19 mm (¾ in) threaded hose adapter

Fountains

Fountains work by drawing water through a pump and discharging it through various types of fountainhead to create different spray effects. The simplest fountains have heads that can be attached directly above the pump. However, to make access easier the pump can be sited away from the fountain and connected by a delivery pipe.

The height and width of the fountain spray or jet depends upon the power of the pump and flow adjuster. For small fountains up to 1.2m (4 ft) high a low-voltage pump should be sufficient. Fountains should be no higher than half the width of the pond to avoid water loss through splashing. Finer sprays will lose more water than bubbling or foaming jets.

Left: This fountainhead produces a 'dandelion head' effect

Lighting

As with all electrical products in the garden, lighting can be either mains or low voltage. It is essential that all light fittings are designed specifically for outdoor use and that underwater lights are specially sealed and designed for immersion. No other type of light fitting should ever be brought into contact with the water.

Low-voltage lighting is adequate for most applications except where a particularly powerful light is required, to uplight a large tree for example. It is particularly flexible, as the cables do not need to be permanently buried. This means that the fittings can be moved around to take advantage of the changing garden scene over the seasons and years. The fixtures themselves are also smaller than mains voltage ones, making them easier to hide within the garden. They will be made from brass, copper, stainless steel or other durable exterior-grade materials; matt black fittings are the least obtrusive.

Low-voltage cable is limited to about 15 m (50 ft) from the transformer in the distance that it can usefully power lighting. Transformers must be designed for outdoor use and located either indoors or under cover, powered by properly installed armoured cables. An internally located transformer makes lighting ponds close to the house easy, but a number of transformers strategically located in the garden allows greater flexibility.

Left: Carefully placed underwater lights illuminate this tiered fountain feature as well as the falling water

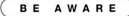

BE AWARE

● Fountains increase water loss through evaporation, so keep pond water levels topped up

● Light fittings can become hot in use; locate them where they cannot be accidentally touched

Useful tips

• Avoid the need to lift hard surfaces by laying ducting pipes before the paving goes down in anticipation of any future cabling

• Consider possible future needs for lighting or further expansion of fountains or filters and install a two- or three-way switch box

• Mark cable runs on a plan for future reference

• Hide pumps, light fittings and cables from view – it is the effect you want to see, not the fixture itself

• Tungsten bulbs are the most common, but it is worth tracking down halogen bulbs which give a brighter light for a given wattage and create a more flattering white light. You can buy various fittings, from spotlights designed to light particular features to underwater lamps and even floating lights. Kits of low-voltage light fittings, cables and a transformer are readily available

Top and above: **A heavy feature, such as a large urn or boulder, will need a more substantial support. A plastic reservoir is installed and concrete blocks set flush with the rim support the feature. The reservoir is then covered with a galvanized steel mesh or grille. A hatch allows access to the pump without removing all the cobbles and the feature**

BE AWARE

● Employ a qualified electrician to install the power supply to your fountain feature

● Always keep the reservoir topped up to ensure that the pump never runs dry

---

Freestanding fountain features

Of all the ways of introducing water into the garden, freestanding reservoir fountain features are among the least expensive and easiest to install. They work on the principle of water being circulated by an electric pump through a fountain feature and returning to a concealed reservoir by gravity. They can be incorporated into any garden setting and as there is no need for any open water they are ideal where child safety is an issue. Furthermore, maintenance is minimized because the covered reservoir reduces the problem of algae and no debris or leaves can find their way in. The range of possibilities is extremely wide, but the feature you choose should suit your style of garden. Various purpose-made plastic or fibreglass reservoirs are available to house the pump, but you could simply use a plastic bin or water tank.

Above: **A large terracotta urn makes an impressive freestanding fountain feature. It is supported on concrete blocks above a reservoir concealed with cobbles (see left). The volume of water spilling over the urn is controlled by the flow adjuster located on the pump. Terracotta is prone to frost damage when wet, so it is important to waterproof inside and out with a proprietary sealant**

A FREESTANDING FOUNTAIN FEATURE

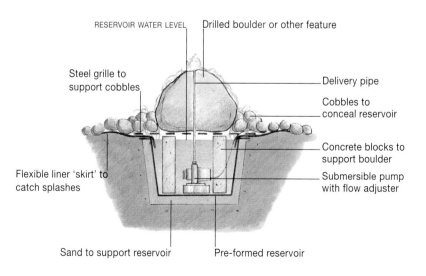

RESERVOIR WATER LEVEL — Drilled boulder or other feature

Steel grille to support cobbles

Delivery pipe

Cobbles to conceal reservoir

Concrete blocks to support boulder

Flexible liner 'skirt' to catch splashes

Submersible pump with flow adjuster

Sand to support reservoir

Pre-formed reservoir

INSTALLING A FREESTANDING FOUNTAIN FEATURE

1 This small fountain feature is available as a complete kit. Measure the width and depth of the reservoir and dig a hole large enough to accommodate it, removing any stones and sharp objects.

2 Spread a layer of sand in and around the hole to support the reservoir and make it easier to level. Place the reservoir into the hole, ensuring that the rim is flush with the surrounding ground.

3 The purpose-made reservoir has a lip to catch water and it is important to keep this perfectly level. Use a spirit level and additional sand to ensure that the rim is level and well supported.

4 Connect the delivery pipe to the pump. In this particular feature, the delivery pipe must be fed through both the lid of the reservoir and the plate that supports the pot feature.

5 Carefully fill the reservoir with water, ensuring that it remains level throughout. Place the pump in the filled reservoir and put the pot in position on the supporting plate.

6 Use a spirit level to check that the pot is level, thus ensuring that the water will flow evenly down all sides. Place coins beneath the pot to make minor adjustments as necessary.

7 Run the water feature to check the flow rate. Changing the setting of the flow adjuster on the pump will allow you to control the volume of water running through the feature.

8 Once you are happy with the effect, the reservoir and pump cable (protected within a length of rigid pipe) can be disguised by placing cobbles around the base of the pot.

9 The completed fountain feature makes an attractive focal point in the garden. It introduces the elements of sound and movement to enliven an adjacent decked seating area. The dark marble cobbles around the base of the pot are particularly attractive when wet and the surrounding low-growing plants integrate the feature into the rest of the garden.

Above: **These beautifully carved lizards mounted on a low wall create a fascinating outlet for this water feature**

Design focus

• If excavation for an underground reservoir is impossible the pump can be housed in the container, although it will be more difficult to conceal the pipe and cable

Below: **Wall-mounted fountains can also be installed adjacent to a pond that effectively acts as the reservoir housing the pump**

Wall-mounted fountain features

Wall fountains are the perfect choice to bring the sound and movement of water into a restricted space, making use of existing walls or other vertical surfaces. They work on the principle of water being circulated by an electric pump from a concealed reservoir to an outlet mounted on a wall. From here the water spills down into a container and back to the reservoir below by means of gravity. As in the case of freestanding fountains, wall-mounted fountains can be incorporated into any garden setting and designed without open water if necessary. The design possibilities are endless, although the water outlet and container should complement each other and suit the style of your garden. Purpose-made plastic or fibreglass containers are available for the reservoir, but again you could use a plastic bin or water tank.

Above: **Plant up around the feature (shown being assembled on the opposite page) to settle it into the garden and disguise the copper delivery pipe with a climbing plant**

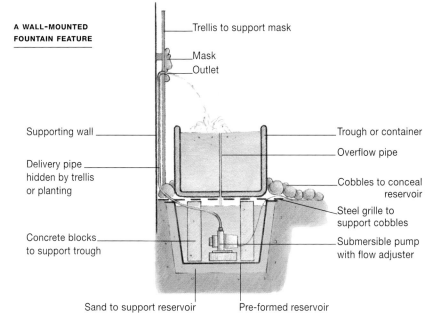

A WALL-MOUNTED FOUNTAIN FEATURE

Trellis to support mask

Mask

Outlet

Supporting wall

Trough or container

Overflow pipe

Delivery pipe hidden by trellis or planting

Cobbles to conceal reservoir

Steel grille to support cobbles

Concrete blocks to support trough

Submersible pump with flow adjuster

Sand to support reservoir

Pre-formed reservoir

INSTALLING A WALL-MOUNTED FOUNTAIN FEATURE

1 Stand the chosen container (in this case a cauldron) in place so you can judge the height at which to set the outlet mask. Record this measurement and mark the position on the wall.

2 Cut a piece of 13 mm (½ in) diameter copper pipe to the correct length and attach it to the wall with special clips. This pipe will deliver water from the reservoir to the mask outlet.

3 Fix short lengths of timber batten to the wall where the mask is to be fixed. These will support the mask and hold it away from the wall, allowing the delivery pipe to run up behind it.

4 Attach a piece of 13 mm (½ in) clear plastic tubing to both ends of a right-angle connector to allow the water to flow from the copper delivery pipe to the mask outlet.

5 Connect one end of the plastic pipe to the copper delivery pipe and feed the other end through the mask outlet (the mouth). The mask can then be fixed in place.

6 Measure the width and depth of the reservoir that will be situated beneath the cauldron, and dig a hole large enough to accommodate it. Remove any stones or sharp objects from the hole.

7 Spread a layer of sand on the bottom of the hole to protect the reservoir and make it easier to level. The galvanized steel grille seen in the background will support the cauldron and cobbles.

8 Place the reservoir into the hole and use a spirit level to ensure that the rim is level and flush with the surrounding ground. Adjust with additional sand as necessary.

9 Using a garden hose, carefully fill the reservoir with water so that it remains stable and level while you back-fill the hole with sand or sifted soil. Tamp down the back-fill as you go.

10 Place concrete blocks in the reservoir to support the galvanized steel grille and the cauldron. Connect the pump to the copper delivery pipe before lowering it into the reservoir.

11 Place the galvanized steel grille and the cauldron in position and fill the cauldron with water. Start the pump and fine-tune the water effect with the flow adjuster on the pump.

12 When you are happy with the effect, disguise the reservoir and pump cable (protected within a rigid pipe) beneath a layer of attractive cobbles placed on top of the grille.

6 • Planting

Above: The strong vertical stems of bulrushes (*Typha* sp.) look dramatic when reflected in water

One of the great advantages of creating ponds and water features is that it allows you the opportunity to grow a whole new range of garden plants. Aquatic plants are some of the easiest to grow successfully and their natural vigour means that it takes very little time to achieve an established look. Plants help to keep the water clear and healthy and many are very beautiful, having colourful flowers, bold leaves or graceful stems which look stunning combined with, and reflected in, water.

Planting design principles

To create a setting for your pond or water feature and link it into the wider garden picture you need to select a range of waterside, moisture-loving and marginal plants. Your choice will depend to a large extent on the effect you are trying to achieve, but as a general rule keep the planting simple and allow the water to remain the focus.

You may select simple sculptural plants to complement a formal pond, subtle colours and textures to enhance an informal one, bold foliage plants to

Below: In this formal garden with its centrally placed bench and calm reflecting pond a simple and restrained planting scheme is required. The four arum lilies (*Zantedeschia* 'Kiwi Blush') are planted symmetrically to reinforce the formality and complement the colour of the bench and terracotta edging tiles

evoke a tropical atmosphere or native plants to attract wildlife. Whatever the style of your pond or water feature, your plants must be chosen with care and consideration; resist the temptation to impulse buy from the garden centre and instead work out your planting scheme in advance with the help of nursery catalogues. Look at foliage combinations as well as flower colours to ensure that your planting is balanced and attractive throughout the year. Check the overall height and spread of each plant to work out how many you need to buy and how far apart they need to be spaced. Plants must also be chosen for their ability to thrive in the type of soil in your garden and their particular location in sun or shade and deep or shallow water (see planting plan, pages 102–3).

Decorative effects are not the only consideration, however. Plants must also

Above: **This informal pond is planted with a range of bright flower colours and foliage textures to create a lush and naturalistic effect. The spiky New Zealand flax (*Phormium tenax* 'Purpureum') has the impact to stand alone while the primulas are planted in drifts of larger numbers to prevent the effect becoming too busy**

fulfil a role in the functional life of the pond, keeping the water clear and healthy. Within the pond you need to include sufficient quantities of those essential plants that will establish a natural balance and prevent the water turning green by arresting the growth of algae. These functional plants can be grouped into submerged (oxygenating) plants, free-floating and floating-leaved plants, and you should include enough to eventually cover up to half of the surface of the pond.

Design focus

• For a restrained and stylish look to a formal pond, place elegant flower and foliage plants singly or symmetrically

• For a lush and naturalistic look to an informal pond, combine foliage shapes and textures in bold swathes

• For a cool, soothing, harmonious effect use blues, mauves, whites and pastel colours

• For a rich, lively, more exotic effect choose reds, oranges, yellows and purples

Pond plants and planting zones

Above: Water lilies (*Nymphaea* sp.) are not only beautiful but their large leaves prevent too much sunlight from reaching the water

FUNCTIONAL PLANTS

Submerged plants (oxygenators) root at the bottom of the pond and oxygenate the water to keep it clear and healthy and able to support other life forms. They are essential for pond creatures, including fish, providing food, spawning sites and shelter. They compete with algae for minerals and sunlight and so help to keep the pond clear of 'green water'.

Free-floating plants float on or just below the surface of the water and provide additional shade to combat the growth of algae. They provide temporary cover before the leaves of more permanent plants emerge.

Floating-leaved plants, such as water lilies, grow in deep water and cover the surface of the water with their leaves.

This provides essential shade to the pond and checks the growth of algae by depriving them of sunlight.

DECORATIVE PLANTS

Marginal plants grow in shallow water or saturated soil around the pond margins. They do not necessarily contribute to good water quality, but they play a valuable role in disguising and stabilizing pond and stream edges as well as providing valuable cover for wildlife. Their diversity of form,

Above: The tiny 'pads' of frogbit (*Hydrocharis morsus-ranae*) and 'pineapple tops' of water soldier (*Stratiotes aloides*) provide shade to check the growth of algae

---

A PROFILE OF THE PLANTED POND

Aquatic plants have specific depth requirements within the pond. The method of planting, either directly into soil or contained within baskets, depends on the style of the pond and the vigour of the individual plant.

To prevent algae, freezing and evaporation becoming problems, ponds should have a minimum depth of 45–60 cm (18–24 in) with marginal planting shelves at 20–25 cm (8–10 in) below water level.

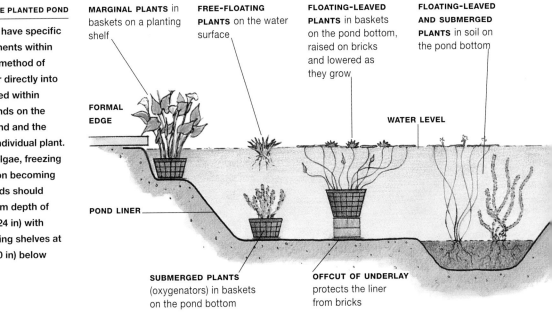

MARGINAL PLANTS in baskets on a planting shelf

FREE-FLOATING PLANTS on the water surface

FLOATING-LEAVED PLANTS in baskets on the pond bottom, raised on bricks and lowered as they grow

FLOATING-LEAVED AND SUBMERGED PLANTS in soil on the pond bottom

FORMAL EDGE

WATER LEVEL

POND LINER

SUBMERGED PLANTS (oxygenators) in baskets on the pond bottom

OFFCUT OF UNDERLAY protects the liner from bricks

foliage and flower creates a frame for the water and contributes to the overall character of the pond.

Moisture-loving plants grow in boggy soil but, unlike marginal plants, require good drainage and will not tolerate being waterlogged. When planted at the water's edge they provide cover for wildlife but their primary function is decorative. Some will also grow in drier soil, making them useful for bridging the gap between water and the rest of the garden and thus integrating the pond into its surroundings.

Waterside plants can be defined as the permanent structure plants such as trees and shrubs that provide a backdrop or context to the pond. Some will create shelter and enclosure while others will stand alone as pondside features, reflecting in the water. Native trees and shrubs will enhance the appearance and habitat potential of wildlife ponds.

Above: Marginal and moisture-loving plants contribute to the overall character of the pond, bringing colour and texture to the margins. Trees and shrubs provide a permanent green backdrop to create a complete garden composition

What are algae?

Algae are microscopic aquatic plants that thrive in bright conditions in clear, nutrient-rich water. They can multiply at an alarming rate, giving rise to 'green water'. They are a naturally occurring part of the pond community and do not actually harm pond life, but they can become a nuisance when conditions favour them over other plants and organisms. Blanket weed is a filamentous form of algae that forms masses of stringy green sheets.

MOISTURE-LOVING PLANTS at the water's edge draw water from the pond via their roots

INFORMAL EDGE

STONE mortared in place to retain soil

MARGINAL PLANTS in soil over a planting shelf, planted according to their specific depth requirements

WATERSIDE PLANTS provide a backdrop and context to the pond

Bog gardens and planted streams

BE AWARE

● The soil surrounding an artificially lined bog garden or stream will be as dry as ordinary garden soil and will not necessarily support moisture-loving plants

Useful tips

• Planting native plants rather than ornamental varieties in the bog garden will make it even more beneficial to wildlife

• Ordinary garden soil can be made more moisture-retentive by adding organic matter (garden compost, well-rotted farmyard manure or leaf mould)

• A mulch of organic matter applied to the soil surface each spring will help to suppress weeds and prevent moisture loss

In nature, bog and marsh are the transition zones between water and dry land. Bog plants require a constant supply of moisture in order to thrive, although some, such as goat's beard (*Aruncus dioicus*) and day lilies (*Hemerocallis* sp.), are very adaptable and will tolerate ordinary garden soil. These plants can provide a visual link between a bog garden or stream and its immediate surroundings. Unless you are lucky enough to have a natural stream that keeps the adjacent soil moist or a permanently damp area of the garden that neither floods in winter nor dries out in summer, you will need to create the conditions for growing bog or moisture-loving plants.

Bog gardens

A bog garden can join a pond to create a comprehensive water garden or it can be separate. Where space for a pond and time for its upkeep is limited or where open water is a hazard to children, a bog garden is an ideal way of creating a lush environment for growing moisture-loving plants. Bog gardens will also attract beneficial insects and amphibians that control garden pests, especially when an area of open water is adjacent. They can be formal or informal in shape depending on the design of your garden. A bog garden can even be created in a container as long as the soil within is kept permanently damp by regular watering but is well drained to prevent stagnation.

A limited bog garden can be created beside a pond or stream if the liner continues beneath the soil beyond the water's edge, allowing plants to soak up moisture from the water through capillary action. In summer, however, this moisture draw can dramatically lower pond water levels and so it is preferable to create an independently watered bog garden. The pond and bog can be separated by a line of stones

Below: **A bog garden can contain some of the most beautiful of all garden plants, such as plantain lily (*Hosta* sp.), false goat's beard (*Astilbe* sp.), umbrella plant (*Darmera peltata*) and iris**

(see diagram, below) or a seamless division can be achieved by concealing the edge with soil (see diagram, below right). Because the two habitats are not actually connected the bog plants can be fed without fear of increasing the nutrient levels in the pond and affecting the natural balance.

Creating a bog garden

After you have marked out the size and shape of the bog garden you will need to dig a hole 45–60 cm (18–24 in) deep; if it is any shallower the bog will dry out in summer. Retain the topsoil for replacement later. Line the hole with a flexible liner, bringing it right up over the edges. Punch drainage holes in the liner at approximately 90 cm (3 ft) intervals with a garden fork and cover

Above: **A massed planting of candelabra primulas (*Primula* sp.) offsets the bold foliage of giant rhubarb (*Rheum palmatum*)**

the bottom with a 5–10 cm (2–4 in) layer of gravel to assist drainage. Incorporate well-rotted organic matter into the retained topsoil to improve its water-retention capacity and refill the hollow. Trim off any surplus liner and conceal the edges with soil, then tread down carefully and water thoroughly.

Plant with moisture-loving plants, taking account of each plant's overall height and spread, general form and shape, foliage texture and flower colour and the direction from which you will be viewing the bog garden. Top up with a garden hose when the soil surface dries (this could be weekly in summer).

Useful tips

• A bog garden can be lined with an offcut of butyl liner, but a less expensive polythene sheet will suffice as the soil will protect it from deterioration by exposure to sunlight

• To make watering easier, incorporate a perforated pipe in the gravel layer. Block one end and connect the other to a garden hose just above ground level, allowing the water to seep out slowly and evenly. Conceal the connector with an evergreen bog plant such as a sedge

AN INDEPENDENT BOG GARDEN

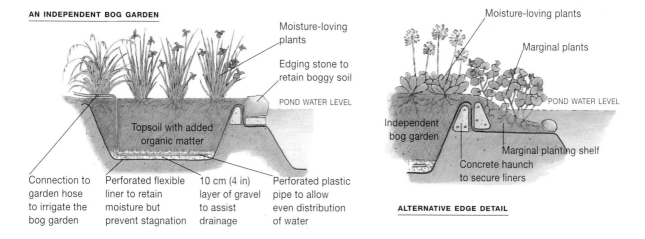

Moisture-loving plants

Edging stone to retain boggy soil

POND WATER LEVEL

Topsoil with added organic matter

Connection to garden hose to irrigate the bog garden

Perforated flexible liner to retain moisture but prevent stagnation

10 cm (4 in) layer of gravel to assist drainage

Perforated plastic pipe to allow even distribution of water

Moisture-loving plants

Marginal plants

POND WATER LEVEL

Independent bog garden

Marginal planting shelf

Concrete haunch to secure liners

ALTERNATIVE EDGE DETAIL

Above: Shallow, moist banks of natural streams are the ideal habitat for moisture-loving plants such as candelabra primulas

Planted streams

If you are planning a stream with the intention of growing moisture-loving plants along its banks, you need to make sure that the stream is graded to create a suitable environment. A shallow V-shaped excavation, lined and covered with topsoil and pebbles, will allow you to grow plants such as primulas, plantain lilies, false goat's beard and ferns at the water's edge. Moving water, together with capillary action, will keep the lower banks moist. If you are creating a stream with rockwork you will need to line a wider U-shaped excavation (see pages 82–5) and remember that the soil beyond the liner will be dry and so unsuitable for moisture-loving plants.

A PLANTED STREAM

Moisture-loving plants benefit from the cool, damp environment at the streamside, drawing up water through their roots.

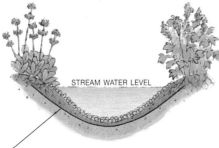

Flexible liner over a V-shaped excavation, covered with soil and pebbles

A waterside planting scheme

This waterside planting plan uses a limited palette to achieve a good balance of leaf shape and flower colour. The fine textures of the groups of iris and grasses complement the broad leaves of plantain lily (*Hosta* sp.) and support the *Gunnera manicata*, which is the star of the show. The smaller plants are used in large groups to keep their overall mass in scale with the larger plants. To increase the natural effect some species have the occasional plant offset from the main group to look as if they have self-seeded. The colours are chosen for their restrained and harmonious effect.

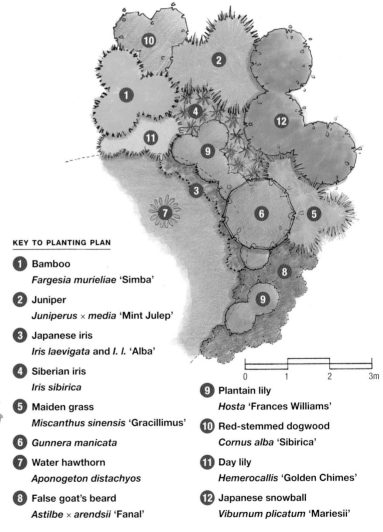

KEY TO PLANTING PLAN

1 Bamboo
Fargesia murieliae 'Simba'

2 Juniper
Juniperus × *media* 'Mint Julep'

3 Japanese iris
Iris laevigata and *I. I.* 'Alba'

4 Siberian iris
Iris sibirica

5 Maiden grass
Miscanthus sinensis 'Gracillimus'

6 *Gunnera manicata*

7 Water hawthorn
Aponogeton distachyos

8 False goat's beard
Astilbe × *arendsii* 'Fanal'

9 Plantain lily
Hosta 'Frances Williams'

10 Red-stemmed dogwood
Cornus alba 'Sibirica'

11 Day lily
Hemerocallis 'Golden Chimes'

12 Japanese snowball
Viburnum plicatum 'Mariesii'

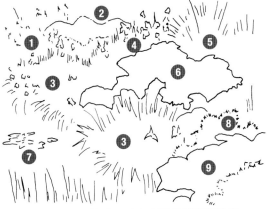

SEE LEFT FOR KEY TO PLANTS SHOWN IN PHOTOGRAPH

Above: The planting scheme aims for a succession of colour and textural interest throughout the year. In spring the cool blue and white irises dominate, giving way to the hotter red false goat's beard and golden day lilies as the season progresses. The backdrop of juniper, bamboo, dogwood and maiden grass creates year-round interest. The plants are spaced according to their estimated spread after 3–5 years

Even though the selection and quantities will be different for a smaller pond you should adopt a similar approach to that described above, with a key plant supported by groups of smaller plants keeping everything in scale

Above: **Bare-rooted plants should have well-developed roots with plenty of finer roots attached**

Above: **Container-grown plants should be well labelled, weed-free, compact and densely foliaged**

Buying and planting

Once you have designed your pond planting scheme you will need to buy your plants. Specialist water garden nurseries often offer better quality plants in a greater range and at lower prices than most general garden centres and are also able to provide more informed advice. Mid to late spring is the ideal time to buy pond plants, but they are usually available all summer and will be sold either bare-rooted or container-grown. The former will be sold to you in plastic bags for planting as soon as you get home. The latter can be left in their containers and submerged in water until you are ready to plant.

Planting time

Planting can take place any time after the danger of frosts has disappeared and the water is warming up. The earlier in the year you plant, the longer the plant has to become established during the growing season. Fill the pond a few days before planting as this will allow the water temperature to reach that of the surrounding atmosphere and give the pond a chance to settle and become more hospitable. Collected rainwater is preferable, but (mineral-rich) tap water is often the only source available in such quantity. You will therefore need to accept the fact that algae may initially occur due to the influx of nutrients. To combat this, add some fast-growing submerged (oxygenating) plants and thin later when the algae problem has subsided.

Planting techniques

There are two ways of planting a pond: either directly into the soil or in baskets or containers (see pond profile, pages 98–9). Planting directly creates a more natural effect and is well suited to larger and wildlife ponds, but because the plants are free to spread they need to be thinned out more frequently. Cover the marginal shelves and the base of the pond with 15 cm (6 in) of soil and plant directly. Planting in baskets controls vigour, protects the liner from sharp roots and makes maintenance easier. Specialist aquatic compost can be purchased, although ordinary garden soil (sifted to remove stones) is perfectly acceptable. Use the fertile top layer taken from your pond excavation.

Far left: **The marginal planting shelf in this pond has been created by mortaring a line of stones to the liner and back-filling with soil (see profile of the planted pond, pages 98–9)**

Left: **A contemporary alternative to the traditional marginal planting shelf**

PLANTING TECHNIQUES

PLANTING directly into the soil can be a tricky business but a stone may be used to hold the plant in place until it has rooted.

PRUNING back the leaves of a newly planted or divided plant can help establishment by reducing the risk of water loss through the leaves.

FLOATING PLANTS such as water soldier (*Stratiotes aloides*) are simply placed on the surface of the water.

SUBMERGED PLANTS can be planted in a container where there is no soil on the bottom of the pond into which they can root.

CONTAINERS AND BASKETS are available in a range of shapes and volumes (*left*). The open lattice-work sides allow water and gases to reach the soil. Baskets with wide-meshed sides need to be lined with a finer-meshed fabric such as hessian to prevent the soil from washing out.

FLOATING-LEAVED PLANTS such as water lilies (*left*) should be planted singly in larger baskets in the deeper parts of the pond. Their stems should just reach the surface, allowing the leaves to float. They can be supported on blocks and gradually lowered as the stems grow.

PLANTING A MARGINAL PLANT

1 Select a basket and cover the bottom with soil or aquatic compost. Remove the plant from its container and place in the basket.

2 Back-fill the basket to just short of the rim and to the original soil level around the plant. Lightly firm down the soil as you fill.

3 Cover the soil with a 1 cm (½ in) layer of gravel. This prevents the soil from floating away and provides extra stability to the basket.

4 Water the plant well and carefully lower it to its preferred depth in the pond, using bricks to raise the basket as necessary.

7 • Plant Selector

On the following pages you will find a selection of the most popular and readily available plants to enhance your pond or water feature.

The Plant Selector begins with the functional plants that are necessary to help maintain water quality (*submerged*, *free-floating* and *floating-leaved plants*). Following these are the more decorative plants that give the pond or water feature its character (*marginal*, *moisture-loving* and *waterside plants*).

The exact height and spread that any plant will attain will inevitably depend upon the particular conditions that are found in your garden. Average dimensions have been given here, along with the preferred water level for planting, where applicable. All the plants listed are hardy to –15°C (5°F) unless otherwise stated.

Key to plant habitat symbols:

Full shade ● Partial shade ◑ Full sun ○

SUBMERGED PLANTS (OXYGENATORS)

These aquatic plants root at the bottom of the pond and have fully or at least partially submerged leaves that release oxygen into the water. Often referred to as 'oxygenators' or 'pond weed', they are vital in maintaining a healthy pond capable of supporting other life forms. They also provide food and spawning sites for adult fish and shelter for fish fry. They are usually supplied in bunches held together with lead clasps which help them to sink and root into the soil at the bottom of the pond. Recommended stocking quantities are 1 bunch per 28–37 cm² (3–4 ft²) of surface area for small ponds up to 4.6 m² (50 ft²) and 1 bunch per 37–46 cm² (4–5 ft²) for ponds over 4.6 m² (50 ft²). They can be planted more densely in new ponds to clear the water of algae quickly but will need to be thinned out when they cover too much surface area and crowd out other plants.

Autumn starwort

Callitriche hermaphroditica, syn. *C. autumnalis*
An excellent oxygenating plant which remains active and in growth throughout winter. The tiny dark green leaves, held on thin branching stems, are entirely submerged. It grows mainly near the bottom of the pond, providing a refuge for underwater creatures and fish fry.
SPREAD indefinite. **PREFERRED WATER LEVEL** 10–50 cm (4–20 in). ○
ALTERNATIVE *C. palustris*, syn. *C. verna* (**water starwort**) has pretty masses of pea-

green starry foliage which dies back during winter. A useful species for shallow ponds and a popular goldfish food plant.

Hornwort

Ceratophyllum demersum
A very hardy submerged perennial with dense whorls of dark green bristly foliage resembling bottle brushes. It makes an excellent oxygenator as well as a refuge for fish fry and is a useful plant as it tolerates shade and grows in very deep water. To establish it, simply drop it into the pool.
SPREAD indefinite. **PREFERRED WATER LEVEL** to 25–150 cm (10–60 in). ○ ●

Fish weed

Lagarosiphon major, syn. *Elodea crispa*
One of the most popular and easily recognizable of all the pondweeds but very vigorous once established. The long, succulent stems are fully submerged and covered in dense whorls of dark green foliage like coiled rope. Almost evergreen and an excellent oxygenator, it is invasive and needs to be kept under control by thinning in summer and cutting back in autumn.
SPREAD indefinite. **PREFERRED WATER LEVEL** to 1.2 m (4 ft). ○

Water violet

Hottonia palustris
A very attractive oxygenating plant with pale lilac flowers held high on erect stems above the water surface in late spring. The bright green ferny foliage forms a delicate

spreading mass below the water surface. It falls to the bottom of the pond in winter and re-emerges the following spring to begin new growth. It is best planted in spring in soil at the bottom of shallow ponds rather than in baskets. Just drop it into the water. In deep water it will float.
HEIGHT 30–60 cm (12–24 in). **SPREAD** indefinite. **PREFERRED WATER LEVEL** to 45 cm (18 in). ○ ◑

Whorled water milfoil

Myriophyllum verticillatum
A rooted perennial plant with delicate bright green needle-like leaves arranged on long, spreading underwater stems. Insignificant yellow-green flowers are borne on spikes held above the water surface in summer. A good oxygenating and fish-spawning plant for smaller ponds and shallow water, where it will spread to soften the pond edges.
HEIGHT 15 cm (6 in). **SPREAD** indefinite. **PREFERRED WATER LEVEL** to 45 cm (18 in). ○ ◑

▼ Fish weed

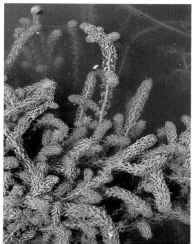

ALTERNATIVE *M. spicatum* (spiked water milfoil) is a similar species with long stems and crimson flower spikes.

Curled pondweed
Potamogeton crispus
The bronze-green submerged leaves are translucent and resemble seaweed. Small crimson and white flowers emerge just above the water surface in summer. It spreads rapidly in mud-bottomed ponds and provides an excellent refuge for fish fry and other organisms. It is more tolerant of shady and cloudy water than other oxygenating plants.
HEIGHT 2.5 cm (1 in). **SPREAD** indefinite.
PREFERRED WATER LEVEL 10–60 cm (4–24 in).
○ ●

Water crowfoot
Ranunculus aquatilis
A shallow-rooting perennial plant with a mass of white and yellow flowers in spring and early summer. These are held above a carpet of rounded surface leaves. The submerged, oxygenating leaves are finely cut and thread-like. It is best in larger, deeper ponds where it can spread and root in mud at the bottom.
HEIGHT 10–15 cm (4–6 in). **SPREAD** indefinite.
PREFERRED WATER LEVEL to 1 m (3¹⁄₄ ft). ○ ●

BE AWARE
Some oxygenating plants are too rampant for the garden pond and have invaded natural watercourses in the countryside, suffocating and displacing native plants and animals. **Stonecrop** (*Chara aspera*), **Canadian pondweed** (*Elodea canadensis*), **parrot's feather** (*Myriophyllum aquaticum*) and *Potamogeton natans* should be used with extreme caution or planted only in container gardens where they can be easily controlled. **Australian stonecrop/ New Zealand pigmyweed** (*Crassula helmsii*, syn. *Tillaea recurva*) should never be introduced.

FREE-FLOATING PLANTS

These plants have leaves, stems and flowers that float on or just below the surface of the water and roots that reach down into it to assimilate plant food. They provide additional shade to the pond, helping to combat algal growth, and are useful in new ponds as they provide cover before the leaves of more permanent plants have developed. To plant, place them gently on the surface of the water.

Water hyacinth
Eichornia crassipes
One of the most beautiful of floating plants, with lavender-blue hyacinth-like flowers which can grow up to 30 cm (12 in) high in warm summers. The round, shiny leaves have swollen stems which keep the plant afloat. It must be brought inside over winter or treated as an annual by obtaining new plants each spring. See Be Aware box (*right*).
HEIGHT 20–30 cm (8–12 in). **SPREAD** indefinite.
PREFERRED WATER LEVEL Shallow or deep water. ○ Half-hardy to 0°C (32°F).

Frogbit
Hydrocharis morsus-ranae
A free-floating perennial plant with bright green circular leaves. Delicate three-petalled white flowers appear in late summer. This species sinks to the bottom of the pond in autumn, reappearing as a young plant in early summer. It prefers still water and is ideal for small ponds and containers. It does best in alkaline conditions.
HEIGHT to 5 cm (2 in). **SPREAD** indefinite.
PREFERRED WATER LEVEL to 30 cm (12 in). ○

Ivy-leaved duckweed
Lemna trisulca
This is the most useful and least invasive of the four species of duckweed. Masses of translucent pale green leaves on thin strands float just below the surface of the water. It encourages the growth of small organisms which help to maintain clear water.
SPREAD indefinite. **PREFERRED WATER LEVEL** Shallow or deep water. ○

▲ **Water soldier**

Water soldier
Stratiotes aloides
A fascinating semi-evergreen foliage plant. Its partly submerged, spiky cactus-like leaves are bright green overlaid with maroon and the late summer flowers are small and white. It sinks to the bottom of the pond after flowering and sends up young plants to the surface in late spring. Being partly submerged it is also a good oxygenator. It needs to be thinned regularly.
HEIGHT 10–20 cm (4–8 in). **SPREAD** indefinite.
PREFERRED WATER LEVEL 30–100 cm (12–39 in). Minimum depth 30 cm (12 in). ○

BE AWARE
Some floating plants can expand so quickly that their foliage excludes all light from the pond, potentially killing its inhabitants. **Lesser duckweed** (*Lemna minor*) and **fairy moss** (*Azolla filiculoides* syn. *caroliniana*) should be used with extreme caution and **floating pennywort** (*Hydrocotyle ranunculoides*) avoided altogether.

Tropical floating plants are often very beautiful and can be used successfully in mini-water gardens in containers. However, they are vigorous and in garden ponds where they are likely to survive the winters they should be avoided. The following have caused serious problems in warm waters throughout the world and have become rampant and problematic weeds: **water hyacinth** (*Eichornia crassipes*), **floating fern** (*Salvinia natans*) and **water lettuce** (*Pistia stratiotes*).

FLOATING-LEAVED PLANTS

These aquatic plants, which include water lilies, grow in deep water and have flowers and large leaves that float on the surface. The leaves prevent too much sunlight reaching the pond, so checking the growth of algae as well as providing shade and shelter for pond life. They can be planted in soil at the bottom of the pond or in large baskets to control their vigour, starting them in shallow water and gradually lowering them to their optimum depth. Recommended stocking quantities are 1 water lily per 4.6 m² (50 ft²) of surface area with the aim of covering a third to a half of the water at maturity.

Water hawthorn
Aponogeton distachyos
An almost evergreen perennial with a different leaf shape and flowering time to the water lilies as well as a greater tolerance of shade. Held on long stems, the bright green oblong leaves float on the surface of the water. The waxy white flowers are sweetly scented and appear on stout stems in spring and again in autumn. In frost-free ponds it may flower during winter. It is best planted in a basket.

▼ Water hawthorn

HEIGHT 10–15 cm (4–6 in). **SPREAD** 1.2 m (4 ft). **PREFERRED WATER LEVEL** 30–60 cm (12–24 in). Frost hardy to –5°C (32°F). ○ ◍

Pond lilies/spatterdocks
Nuphar **SPECIES AND VARIETIES**
Pond lilies are related to water lilies but are more tolerant of deeper, running water and shade, where in such conditions they can be used as a substitute. The golden-yellow flowers are relatively small and spherical and are held above the surface in summer. The large, leathery floating leaves are spade or heart-shaped and the underwater foliage is often beautifully translucent. Because of their vigour, pond lilies are best suited to larger ponds and are planted where conditions are not those required by the more decorative water lilies. They can be contained in large baskets.
HEIGHT 10–15 cm (4–6 in). **SPREAD** to 1.5 m (5 ft). **PREFERRED WATER LEVEL** 30–60 cm (12–24 in). ○ ◍
N. advena (**American spatterdock**) has yellow flowers tinged bronze with bright red stamens. *N. japonica* (**Japanese pond lily**) is a smaller species (spread to 90 cm/ 3 ft) requiring stiller water and more sun to flower freely. *N. j.* **var**. *rubrotinctum* is a variety with orange-red flowers. *N. lutea* (**brandy bottle/yellow pond lily**) is a larger species (spread to 2.4 m/8 ft) with bottle-shaped, brandy-scented flowers. It can be planted in deeper water (to 2.4 m/8 ft) but is only suitable for the largest of ponds. *N. pumila* (**dwarf pond lily**) is suitable for medium-sized ponds (preferred water level 30–45 cm/ 12–18 in).

Water fringe
Nymphoides peltata
A creeping aquatic plant with leaves resembling miniature water lily pads. Clusters of small, funnel-shaped yellow flowers are produced successively throughout the summer, held above the water. The small, heart-shaped floating leaves are bright green blotched maroon. It can grow rapidly in still or moving water

▲ Water lily 'Firecrest'

and will need to be thinned occasionally. Plant in a basket to control its vigour.
HEIGHT 5–10 cm (2–4 in). **SPREAD** 60 cm (2 ft). **PREFERRED WATER LEVEL** 15–45 cm (6–18 in). ○

Water lilies
Nymphaea **SPECIES AND VARIETIES**
Water lilies are the most popular and evocative of all aquatic plants and no pond is complete without at least one. There is a variety for every size of pond and depth of water and a flower colour to suit all tastes. The beautiful cup- or star-shaped flowers float on the surface of the water and appear throughout the summer, opening in the morning and closing as evening approaches. Many are scented and the colours range from pure white through to pink, red, orange and yellow, and even blue in the case of some tropical species. The roots and stems are submerged and the leaves (pads), which lie flat on the water surface, provide valuable shade to the pond. All lilies need a sunny, sheltered position and still water. Growth can be controlled and maintenance made easier by planting lilies in baskets.
SPREAD (generally) 1.2–1.5 m (4–5 ft). **PREFERRED WATER LEVEL** (generally) 15–100 cm (6–36 in), depending on variety/species. ○

White-flowered lilies
Nymphaea **'Marliacea Albida'** is a popular and free-flowering white lily for medium to

large ponds. The large, semi-double, cup-shaped flowers are fragrant and appear from early In the season. The flower has yellow stamens and the young bronze foliage matures to deep green pads.
ALTERNATIVES *N.* **'Gonnère'** has fully double scented white flowers and pea-green pads. *N.* **'Virginalis'** is a long-flowering pure white lily with scented shell-shaped petals. *N.* *alba* is a huge, vigorous species tolerant of much greater depths (30–90 cm/12–36 in) and should only be grown in large ponds. *N. odorata* var. *minor* is a small, fragrant, white-flowered lily (spread 60–90 cm/2–3 ft) with pale green leaves for small ponds (preferred water level 15–30 cm/6–12 in), tubs and containers.

Pink-flowered lilies
Nymphaea **'Pink Sensation'** is one of the finest free-flowering pink lilies for medium to large ponds. The star-shaped clear pink flowers have yellow stamens and stay open late into the afternoon. The leaves open purple, becoming deep green as they mature.
ALTERNATIVES *N.* **'Firecrest'** has fragrant, star-shaped pink flowers tipped crimson held just above the surface of the water. *N.* **'Rose Arey'** has fragrant, perfectly star-shaped rose-pink flowers with bright orange-yellow stamens. *N.* **'Laydekeri Lilacea'** has very fragrant small lilac-pink flowers and is suitable for smaller ponds (preferred water level 30–45 cm/12–18 in), tubs and containers. *N.* **'Laydekeri Rosea'** is another

▼ Water lily 'Escarboucle'

▲ Water lily 'Marliacea Chromatella'

lily for smaller ponds, tubs and containers, bearing scented, deep rose-pink flowers.

Red-flowered lilies
Nymphaea **'Escarboucle'** is one of the most outstanding red lilies available and is suitable for medium to larger ponds. The large semi-double flowers are a uniform shade of bright crimson with gold stamens and stay open late in the afternoon. The young bronze-tinged leaves mature to deep green pads.
ALTERNATIVES *N.* **'James Brydon'** has rich crimson double flowers and is suitable for large and small ponds but not for tubs and containers. *N.* **'René Gerard'** has large rose-pink star-shaped flowers streaked crimson towards the centre and bronze foliage maturing to green pads up to 30 cm (12 in) in diameter. *N.* **'William Falconer'** has blood-red flowers and dark purple foliage and can be grown in deep water (preferred water level 45–75 cm/18–30 in). *N.* **'Froebelii'** is smaller with deep red flowers, orange stamens and small round leaves and is ideal for shallow ponds (preferred water level 15–30 cm/6–12 in), tubs and containers.

Yellow-flowered lilies
Nymphaea **'Marliacea Chromatella'** is the best all-round yellow lily for any size of pond. The large semi-double primrose-yellow flowers have orange stamens and are borne in great profusion. The coppery young leaves mature to green and purple mottled pads.
ALTERNATIVES *N.* **'Odorata Sulpharea'** has fragrant star-shaped sulphur-yellow flowers but needs a warm spot to flower well. *N.* **'Pygmaea Helvola'** is a miniature lily (spread 60 cm/2 ft) with small yellow flowers and purple mottled leaves. Ideal for small shallow ponds (preferred water level 15–30 cm/6–12 in), tubs and containers.

Lilies with flowers of changeable colour
Nymphaea **'Comanche'** is a lily for any slze of pond. The large flower petals open coppery-yellow and change through to coppery-red. The stamens are orange and the large leaves are olive green speckled with brown.
ALTERNATIVES *N.* **'Aurora'** is a smaller lily (spread 75 cm/2½ ft) whose semi-double flowers change from creamy-yellow to pinkish-orange to ruby red, with orange stamens. *N.* **'Indiana'** is another small lily (spread 75 cm/2½ ft) with apricot-yellow flowers changing to copper-red. It is ideal for shallow ponds (preferred water level 15–30 cm/6–12 in), tubs and containers.

Blue-flowered (tropical) lilies
Nymphaea **'Blue Beauty'** is a free-flowering tropical water lily for any size of pond. The fragrant semi-double flowers have deep blue petals and golden-yellow stamens. The large, deep green leaves are flecked brown above and have slightly wavy edges. It can be successfully planted in tubs and containers and moved to frost-free conditions over winter (minimum water temperature 10°C/50°F). It is half hardy to 0°C (32°F).
ALTERNATIVE *N.* *capensis* (**Cape blue water lily**) is a larger lily (spread 2.4 m/8 ft) with huge leaves and light blue flowers with yellow stamens held above the water.

Golden club
Orontium aquaticum
An impressive perennial grown for its bold leaves and strange poker-like flowers. The large, waxy blue-green leaves have silver undersides and float on the water surface. The narrow white flower spikes are tipped with gold florets and appear in spring. It should not be planted in baskets but grown in deeper water in at least 30 cm (12 in) of soil. It hates disturbance once planted.
HEIGHT 30–45 cm (12–18 in). **SPREAD** 45–60 cm (18–24 in). **PREFERRED WATER LEVEL** 10–45 cm (4–18 in). ◯

MARGINAL PLANTS

These aquatic plants grow in shallow water or the saturated soil around the pond margins. Some contribute to water quality by removing excess nutrients through their roots and others will spread and help to stabilize and disguise the pond edges. Many are beautiful in form and flower and their most important contribution is to the visual appearance of the pond or water feature. In formal ponds they can be planted in baskets on marginal shelves to control their vigour. In informal and wildlife ponds they can be planted directly into soil in the margins to give a more natural edge and provide valuable cover for wildlife. Many, for example arrowhead and bog bean, will grow and spread quickly, so only a limited number are required. Each should be planted according to its required depth of water.

Sweet rush
Acorus calamus
A vigorous, upright foliage plant for the margins of large ponds and stream banks. The green sword-like leaves have wavy edges and are aromatic when crushed. Small brown conical flowers emerge above the leaf tips in summer.
HEIGHT 75–90 cm (2¹/₂ ft–3 ft). **SPREAD** 90 cm (3 ft) plus. **PREFERRED WATER LEVEL** 8–25 cm (3–10 in). ○
ALTERNATIVES *A. c.* **'Variegatus'** is a less invasive variety with green leaves striped cream-yellow, more suited to smaller ponds. *A. gramineus* (**Japanese rush**) is a dwarf species (15 cm/6 in) with tufts of green grassy foliage for small ponds (to 2.5 cm/1 in) and container gardens.

Water plantain
Alisma plantago-aquatica
A frothy-flowered perennial for shallow water around larger wildlife ponds and streams. Tiny pinkish-white flowers are held on tall stems above handsome rosettes of broad, oval leaves in summer.
HEIGHT 75–90 cm (2¹/₂–3 ft). **SPREAD** 45 cm (18 in). **PREFERRED WATER LEVEL** 15–24 cm (6–10 in). ○

Flowering rush
Butomus umbellatus
An elegant summer-flowering plant with rose-pink flower umbels like starbursts carried high above slender olive-green leaves. Slow-spreading, it grows best in open ground rather than in a planting basket.
HEIGHT 75–120 cm (2¹/₂–4 ft). **SPREAD** 45cm (18 in). **PREFERRED WATER LEVEL** 5–30 cm (2–12 in). ○ ◉

▲ **Flowering rush**

Bog arum
Calla palustris
This creeping perennial will root in the mud and mask the edge of the pond. The plant has glossy green heart-shaped leaves and pure white arum-like flowers in spring. Clusters of bright red berries appear on the female plants by late summer.
HEIGHT 15–25 cm (6–10 in). **SPREAD** 30 cm (12 in) plus. **PREFERRED WATER LEVEL** 5–25 cm (2–10 in). ○ ◉

Marsh marigold
Caltha palustris
A popular early-flowering groundcover plant. The golden-yellow buttercup-like flowers are freely produced throughout spring and show well against mounds of rich green leaves.
HEIGHT 45–60 cm (18–24 in). **SPREAD** 45cm (18 in). **PREFERRED WATER LEVEL** to 10 cm (4 in). ○ ◉
ALTERNATIVES *C. p.* **'Flore Plena'** is a slightly smaller double-flowered variety. *C. p.* **var. alba** is a more compact plant with white flowers and prefers damp soil.

Ornamental rush
Cyperus longus
An impressive but invasive grass-like perennial for larger ponds. The long, thin,

◀ **Marsh marigold**

ribbed leaves are deep green and quickly spread to form large grassy masses. The elegant red-brown flower heads, which appear in late summer and last well into winter, are popular with flower arrangers. The plant emits a sweet scent from its stems and roots.

HEIGHT 60–90 cm (2–3 ft). **SPREAD** 90 cm (3 ft). **PREFERRED WATER LEVEL** 5–25 cm (2–10 in). ○ **ALTERNATIVE** *C. papyrus* is an evergreen sedge with fine pendulous leaves and masses of dramatic flower sprays over 3 m (10 ft) high. It is frost tender (to 0°C/32°F) but can be grown in a container water garden and moved to a frost-free location over winter.

Cotton grass
Eriophorum angustifolium
A vigorous, evergreen grassy plant for marsh or larger pond margins; silky white cotton wool-like flowers appear in early summer above dense, spiky tufts of grass-like leaves. It grows best in peaty, acidic soil.

HEIGHT 30–45 cm (12–18 in). **SPREAD** indefinite. **PREFERRED WATER LEVEL** to 5 cm (2 in). ○

Variegated water grass
Glyceria maxima var. *variegata*
A strong-growing aquatic grass to provide groundcover at the water's edge. The broad grassy leaves are striped creamy-white, flushed pink in spring. Creamy-green flower heads appear well above the foliage in summer. Planting in a basket will control the vigour of this plant and protect the pond liner from its sharp roots.

HEIGHT 60–75 cm (2–2¹/₂ ft). **SPREAD** indefinite. **PREFERRED WATER LEVEL** to 15 cm (6 in). ○

Houttuynia cordata
This is an attractive and quickly spreading groundcover plant for the water's edge. The bluish-green heart-shaped leaves are tinged purple and emit a strong, orangey scent when bruised. Four-petalled white flowers are held high on bright red stems in summer.

HEIGHT 15–60 cm (6–24 in). **SPREAD** indefinite.

▲ **Variegated water grass**

PREFERRED WATER LEVEL to 10 cm (4 in). ○ ◐ Frost hardy to –5°C (23°F). **ALTERNATIVES** *H. c.* '**Flore Pleno**' is a double-flowered form. *H. c.* '**Chameleon**', syn. *H. c.* '**Variegata**', has green leaves splashed red and yellow.

Marsh St John's wort
Hypericum elodes
A dainty trailing plant useful for growing on pond margins to disguise the edges. It has small pale green leaves and clusters of soft yellow flowers in summer.

HEIGHT 5–10 cm (2–4 in). **SPREAD** indefinite. **PREFERRED WATER LEVEL** to 10 cm (4 in). ○

Japanese iris
Iris laevigata
One of the finest water irises for the garden pond. Clear, three-petalled sky-blue flowers appear in June and often again in September. The clumps of smooth, sword-shaped leaves are a soft, pale green. Plant en masse in the muddy shallows for maximum impact.

HEIGHT 60–90 cm (2–3 ft). **SPREAD** indefinite. **PREFERRED WATER LEVEL** to 10 cm (4 in). ○ **ALTERNATIVES** *I. l.* '**Alba**' is a white variety. *I. l.* '**Snowdrift**' is a double-flowered white form. *I. l.* '**Variegata**' has blue flowers and green and silver-white foliage. *I. l.* '**Colchesterensis**' has double white flowers heavily mottled violet-blue.

Yellow flag
Iris pseudacorus
Yellow flag is a sturdy and vigorous iris suited to the margins of larger and wildlife ponds. The rigid sword-like leaves are grey-green and can be up to 1.2 m (4 ft) tall. Strong stems support large butter-yellow flowers with deeper yellow fall petals in early summer. The flowers are followed by plenty of good seed heads.

HEIGHT 90–120 cm (3–4 ft). **SPREAD** indefinite. **PREFERRED WATER LEVEL** to 10 cm (4 in). ○ ◐ **ALTERNATIVES** *I. p. bastardii* is a smaller, less vigorous form with paler yellow flowers. *I. p.* '**Variegata**' is a less vigorous variety with foliage edged cream in spring.

Blue flag
Iris versicolor
An elegant and colourful long-flowering iris for the pond margins and wet soil. The narrow leaves are grey-green and the summer flowers are violet-blue with fall petals veined purple, yellow and white.

HEIGHT 45–60 cm (18–24 in). **SPREAD** indefinite. **PREFERRED WATER LEVEL** to 7.5 cm (3 in). ○ **ALTERNATIVES** *I. v.* '**Kermesina**' has broader leaves and rich claret-red foliage.

▼ **Japanese iris**

Corkscrew rush

Juncus effusus var. *spiralis*
This curious oddity for the water's edge is also popular with flower arrangers. The semi-rigid leafless stems twist and curl to form spirals and dense, green-brown flower tufts appear in midsummer. It makes a good specimen for a container water garden.
HEIGHT 30–60 cm (12–24 in). **SPREAD** 60 cm (2 ft). **PREFERRED WATER LEVEL** to 7.5 cm (3 in). ◯

Yellow skunk cabbage

Lysichiton americanus
A vigorous and impressive plant for the larger bog garden or informal pond in still or moving water. Magnificent yellow arum-like flowers 30 cm/12in high appear in early spring, followed by massive, leathery, weed-suppressing leaves. This plant needs deep, rich soil and constant moisture to grow well.
HEIGHT 60–90 cm (2–3 ft). **SPREAD** 60–90 cm (2–3 ft). **PREFERRED WATER LEVEL** to 10 cm (4 in). ◯ ●
ALTERNATIVE *L. camtschatcensis* is a slightly smaller Japanese species with scented white flowers.

Water mint

Mentha aquatica
A vigorous, low-spreading perennial for the water's edge. It has small, green-purple

▲ Yellow skunk cabbage

aromatic foliage and pale mauve flowers in summer. Like all mints, it spreads rapidly and should be divided regularly.
HEIGHT 60–90 cm (2–3 ft). **SPREAD** usually less than 90 cm (3 ft). **PREFERRED WATER LEVEL** to 15 cm (6 in). ◯ ●

Bog bean

Menyanthes trifoliata
This attractive low-growing plant with trailing stems makes a contrast to the more vertical marginal plants. Tiny white star-like flowers open from pink buds in late spring above clover-like leaves held on trailing stalks.
HEIGHT 15–20 cm (6–8 in). **SPREAD** indefinite. **PREFERRED WATER LEVEL** 5–10 cm (2–4 in). ◯

Water forget-me-not

Myosotis scorpioides syn. *M. palustris*
A low creeping plant for the muddy shallows and useful for disguising pond edges. Bright blue flowers are freely produced during spring and summer over sprawling mounds of narrow, glossy green foliage. It can easily be reduced if it becomes too vigorous.

HEIGHT 30 cm (12 in). **SPREAD** 60 cm (2 ft). **PREFERRED WATER LEVEL** to 10 cm (4 in). ◯
ALTERNATIVE *M. s.* 'Mermaid' has larger flowers of a more intense blue.

Green arrow arum

Peltandra undulata, syn. *P. virginica*
A stately aquatic plant with clumps of bold foliage and flowers. Narrow greenish-white arum-like flowers appear in summer, followed by clusters of green berries. The upright leaves are bright green and arrow-shaped.
HEIGHT 75 cm ($2\frac{1}{2}$ ft). **SPREAD** 45 cm (18 in). **PREFERRED WATER LEVEL** to 25 cm (10 in). ◯

Pickerel weed

Pontederia cordata
An essential and robust water plant providing bold foliage and late summer colour. Compact spikes of soft blue flowers are produced above dense clumps of smooth, lance-shaped leaves. Plant in a group for maximum impact.
HEIGHT 60–75 cm (2–$2\frac{1}{2}$ ft). **SPREAD** 45 cm (18 in). **PREFERRED WATER LEVEL** 10–30 cm (4–12 in), best at 25–30 cm (10–12 in). ◯
ALTERNATIVE *P. c. alba* is a variety bearing white flowers.

Arrowhead

Sagittaria sagittifolia syn. *S. japonica*
A short-branching spreading plant with fresh green architectural foliage. Small three-petalled white flowers with dark centres appear in summer but the distinctive arrow-shaped leaves are the main attraction. The underwater foliage is a useful oxygenator. It can be contained in a planting basket to control its vigour.
HEIGHT 45–60 cm (18–24 in). **SPREAD** 45–60 cm (18–24 in) **PREFERRED WATER LEVEL** to 20 cm (8 in), but will grow in water up to 60 cm (2 ft). ◯
ALTERNATIVES *S. s.* 'Flore Pleno' has double white flowers and is less invasive.
S. latifolia is a more imposing American species and is better for deeper water (15–30 cm/6–12 in).

▼ Bog bean

▶ **Arum lily**

Zebra rush

Schoenoplectus lacustris subsp.
tabernaemontani 'Zebrinus'
This striking ornamental rush has tall,
rounded stems distinctively banded cream
and green. Brown and white flower spikes
appear in summer. Allow the plant to creep
into fresh soil or it will need lifting and
dividing every other year to maintain the
conspicuous stripes. An essential water plant
for adding height and drama, it is suitable for
all pond sizes.
HEIGHT to 1.5 m (5 ft). **SPREAD** 60 cm (2 ft).
PREFERRED WATER LEVEL to 30 cm (12 in). ◯
ALTERNATIVE *S. t.* '**Albescens**' is slightly taller
with green and white vertically striped stems.

Reedmace

Typha laxmanii
Possibly the most beautiful of 'bulrushes',
this species has very narrow pale green
leaves. The characteristic 'bulrush' flower

▼ **Zebra rush**

heads are ginger-brown in colour and held
on tall, graceful stems. Planting in a basket
will control the vigour of these plants and
protect the pond liner from the sharply
pointed roots.
HEIGHT 90–120 cm (3–4 ft). **SPREAD** indefinite.
PREFERRED WATER LEVEL to 15 cm (to 6 in).
◯ ◉
ALTERNATIVES *T. minima* is a less invasive,
fine-leaved dwarf species (15 cm/6 in)
for smaller ponds (preferred water level to
15 cm/6 in). *T. angustifolia* (**lesser
reedmace**) is a vigorous species for larger
ponds. *T. latifolia* (**great reedmace**) is an
extremely vigorous 'bulrush' for the margins
of lakes or very large ponds only.

Brooklime

Veronica beccabunga
This species is a semi-evergreen creeping
plant with tiny blue flowers that are
produced throughout the summer. The
luxuriant fleshy foliage is free-spreading and
therefore useful for disguising the pond
edges. It can be controlled by planting in
a basket.

HEIGHT 10–20 cm (4–8 in). **SPREAD** indefinite.
PREFERRED WATER LEVEL to 10 cm (4 in). ◯

Arum lily

Zantedeschia aethiopica
A handsome summer-flowering tuberous
plant with elegant flowers and foliage, arum
lily is well suited to planting in formal ponds.
The scented, pure white flowers are funnel-
shaped with a distinctive central yellow
spike and are produced in succession
throughout the summer. The arrow-shaped
leaves are a dark glossy green. It will also
grow in moist, well-drained soil but will
more reliably survive winter frosts if
covered with 10–30 cm (4–12 in) of water.
Alternatively, remove to frost-free quarters
over winter.
HEIGHT to 60 cm (2 ft). **SPREAD** to 40 cm
(16 in). **PREFERRED WATER LEVEL** 5–25 cm
(2–10 in). ◯ Half-hardy to 0°C° (32°F).
ALTERNATIVES *Z. a.* '**Crowborough**' is a
slightly smaller but hardier form. *Z. a.* '**Green
Goddess**' has green flowers splashed white.
Z. '**Kiwi Blush**' has white flowers flushed
pink at the base.

MOISTURE-LOVING PLANTS

These plants thrive in the moist soil at the edge of the pond, alongside streams and in bog gardens. Sometimes referred to as 'bog plants', they differ from marginal plants as they need good drainage and do not tolerate being waterlogged. Their primary function is decorative, offering massive stature, bold foliage or colourful flowers. Planted beyond the water's edge, they can help to connect the pond visually with the rest of the garden. Plant larger specimen plants individually; smaller plants look better in groups of three or more. Many will grow in ordinary garden soil but will be more lush and vigorous where adequate moisture is available.

Goat's beard
Aruncus dioicus
This handsome flowering perennial plant has dense clumps of weed-suppressing foliage. The broad, fern-like leaves are often bronze green in spring, becoming pale green in summer. Elegant, creamy-white flower plumes (more feathery on male plants) appear in early summer. Moist ground is ideal but the plant will tolerate most soils.

▲ Bowles' golden sedge

HEIGHT 1.2–1.8 m (4–6 ft). **SPREAD** 90–120 cm (3–4 ft). ○ ▦
ALTERNATIVE *A. d.* **'Kneiffii'** is smaller (60–90 cm/2–3 ft) with finely cut leaves.

False goat's beard
Astilbe **SPECIES AND VARIETIES**
This is a genus of highly attractive moisture-loving perennials in a wide range of flower colours. Feathery plumes of white, pink or red flowers appear in summer, the brown flower heads remaining attractive throughout winter. The pretty toothed leaves make good groundcovering clumps. Only plant in full sun if abundant moisture is available. Plant en masse at the water's edge for a spectacular summer show.
HEIGHT 60–75 cm (2–2¹/₂ ft). **SPREAD** 45 cm (18 in). ▦
A. × arendsii **'Fanal'** has deep red flowers and dark green leaves. *A. × a.* **'Snowdrift'** has white flowers and bright green leaves. *A. × a.* **'Venus'** is a taller variety with shell-pink flowers and dark foliage. *A. simplicifolia* **'Bronze Elegans'** is a later-flowering species only 30 cm (12 in) high with clear pink flowers and bronze-tinted foliage.

Bowles' golden sedge
Carex elata 'Aurea', syn. *C. stricta* 'Bowles' Golden'
A bright, low-growing evergreen sedge that makes a contrast to other foliage plants at the water's edge, this plant forms dense graceful tussocks of grassy golden-yellow foliage with green margins. Brown-black flower spikes are held among the leaves in summer. Boggy soils and full sun are the ideal conditions; the leaf colour is a more subdued lime-green in shade.
HEIGHT 45–60 cm (18–24 in). **SPREAD** 45–60 cm (18–24 in). ○ Hardy.
ALTERNATIVE *C. oshimensis* **'Evergold'** is a slightly lower, more rounded plant with wider yellow-striped leaves.

Weeping sedge
Carex pendula
A graceful and spreading evergreen sedge for the shadier parts of large and wildlife ponds. Long, pendulous brown flowers are supported on tall, arching stems beyond the grassy green foliage in summer. It is a versatile plant that will also grow in shallow water and drier soils, thereby blurring the edges of the water garden, but it can seed

◀ False goat's beard 'Fanal'

▲ Umbrella plant

itself too readily in some situations.
HEIGHT 60–90 cm (2–3 ft). **SPREAD** 90–120 cm (3–4 ft). ◐

Umbrella plant
Darmera peltata
This is an impressive foliage plant for rich, boggy soil beside a large informal pool or stream. Flat, circular heads of pink and white flowers appear on bare, erect stems before the leaves develop in spring. By summer the leaves are large, round and scalloped, like inverted parasols, often 30 cm (12 in) in diameter. In autumn they take on colourful tints of copper and maroon. The creeping roots are useful for protecting pond edges from erosion but are invasive.
HEIGHT 90–120 cm (3–4 ft). **SPREAD** 1.2 m (4 ft). ○ ◐

Joe Pye weed
Eupatorium purpureum
A coarse but impressive upright perennial for moist soils beside the larger water garden. Large flat, fluffy heads of pinkish-purple flowers are borne on stout purplish stems in late summer to early autumn. Dark green oval leaves are arranged around the stems lower down.
HEIGHT 1.8–2.4 m (6–8 ft). **SPREAD** 90–120 cm (3–4 ft). ○ ◐
ALTERNATIVE *E. p.* **subsp.** *maculatum* **'Atropurpureum'** has rosy-purple flowers.

Dropwort
Filipendula purpurea
A graceful flowering and foliage plant for group planting at the water's edge. Dense branched heads of rose-pink, fragrant flowers which appear to sit on the foliage in summer are followed by bronze seed heads. The attractive clumps of deeply divided leaves make good groundcover in rich, moist soils which do not dry out.
HEIGHT 90–120 cm (3–4 ft). **SPREAD** 60–90 cm (2–3 ft). ◐
ALTERNATIVE *F. ulmaria* 'Aurea' (**meadowsweet**) is a slightly smaller species with creamy-white flowers and attractive golden-green leaves.

Avens
Geum **SPECIES AND VARIETIES**
Small and cheerful semi-evergreen perennials for moist soils at the water's edge. Nodding sprays of cup-shaped orange or yellow flowers are held on slender hairy stems above the foliage throughout summer. The attractive clumps of hairy, lobed leaves make dense groundcover.
HEIGHT 45–60 cm (18–24 in). **SPREAD** 45 cm (18 in). ○ ◐
G. **'Borisii'** is a smaller and neater species with single orange flowers. G. **'Lady Stratheden'** has double bright yellow flowers. G. **'Mrs J. Bradshaw'** has double scarlet-red flowers. G. *rivale* **'Leonard's Variety'** is an earlier-flowering species with coppery-pink flowers, growing best in boggy ground.

Gunnera manicata
An enormous foliage plant to use as a specimen adjacent to a large pond or stream. The huge, rough, lobed leaves expand from thick stems, reaching up to 1.8 m (6 ft) diameter in rich, boggy ground. Huge, green, conical flower spikes appear in spring and turn rust-red as the season progresses. Protect the crowns and leaf buds from frost over winter with mulch or compost or by folding in the plant's decaying leaves.

HEIGHT 1.8–3 m (6–10 ft). **SPREAD** 1.8–3 m (6–10 ft). ◯ ◐ Frost hardy (to –5°C/23°F).
ALTERNATIVES G. *chilensis* is hardier and slightly smaller (1.8 m/6 ft) with more rounded and puckered leaves. It is better for smaller gardens. G. *magellanica* is a completely different plant growing no more than 5–7.5 cm (2–3 in) and useful for groundcover in damp, shady areas.

Day lilies
Hemerocallis **SPECIES AND VARIETIES**
These are tough and trouble-free flowering perennials for massed waterside planting. The lily-like trumpet flowers last only one day but are borne in long succession throughout the summer above arching mounds of strap-like semi-evergreen leaves, which over time form large, weed-suppressing clumps. Plant

▼ *Gunnera chilensis*

in rich, moisture-retentive soils and light shade for the best results.

HEIGHT 60–75 cm (2–2¹/₂ ft). **SPREAD** 45–60 cm (18–24 in). ◯ ◖

H. **'Burning Daylight'** has fragrant orange flowers. *H.* **'Stafford'** is slightly taller with deep red flowers and orange yellow throats. *H.* **'Golden Chimes'** is shorter (45 cm/18 in) with masses of golden-yellow flowers. *H.* **lilio-asphodelus** is a species with very fragrant, delicate lemon-yellow flowers.

Plantain lilies
Hosta SPECIES AND VARIETIES

Handsome foliage plants for specimen planting or for providing a textural contrast to other waterside plants. Large, elegant, oval to heart-shaped leaves, often beautifully variegated, form neat clumps of ground-covering foliage. Mauve, lilac or white tubular flowers are held graciously above the foliage in summer. The leaves are very prone to slug damage and need to be protected.

HEIGHT 45–75 cm (18–30 in). **SPREAD** 60–150 cm (2–5 ft). ● ◖

H. **fortunei** var. **albopicta** has pale yellow leaves edged green and mauve flowers. The leaves of *H. f.* **aureomarginata** are green edged creamy yellow and the flowers are mauve. *H.* **'Halcyon'** is a small variety (30 cm/12 in) with elegant silver-grey leaves and smoky lilac flowers. *H.* **'Royal Standard'** has rich green leaves and white flowers; *H.* **'Thomas Hogg'** has smooth green leaves with creamy margins and pale lilac flowers. *H.* **sieboldiana** is a magnificent blue-leaved hosta for specimen planting or mass groundcover beside larger pools. This species has impressive heart-shaped leaves which are bluish-green and deeply ribbed, growing up to 30 cm (12 in) in diameter in rich, moist soils. Palest lilac, trumpet-shaped flowers appear just above the foliage in early summer. This species will tolerate some sun but the leaves will become a dull green. It reaches a height of 60–75 cm (2–2¹/₂ ft) and spread of 1.2–1.5 m (4–5 ft). *H. s.* **var.**

▶ *Hosta sieboldiana*

▲ *Inula hookeri*

elegans has even larger, bluer leaves. *H.* **'Frances Williams'**, derived from the same species, has creamy yellow margins to the leaves and should not be grown in full sun.

Inula hookeri

A bushy perennial offering late summer colour for rich, moist soil or the wilder bog garden, this plant has pale yellow daisy-like flowers which open from woolly buds in mid to late summer and have very distinctive, ray-like petals. The spreading clumps of lance-shaped hairy leaves can be invasive.

HEIGHT 60–75 cm (2–2¹/₂ ft). **SPREAD** 60–75 cm (2–2¹/₂ ft). ◯ ◖

ALTERNATIVE *I.* **magnifica** is a taller species (1.5–1.8 m/5–6ft) with golden-yellow flowers.

Japanese iris
Iris ensata, syn. *I. kaempferi*

This majestic Japanese iris can be planted en masse for maximum impact. Beardless violet-purple flowers appear in summer above dense clumps of narrow sword-shaped leaves. It is a difficult plant to grow in that it has very specific requirements, needing full sun and lime-free soil that stays damp throughout the summer.

HEIGHT 60–75 cm (2–2¹/₂ ft). **SPREAD** indefinite. ◯

ALTERNATIVES *I. e.* **'Variegata'** has green and white variegated leaves. *I. e.* **Higo hybrids** are slightly taller, with a range of flower colours of blue, purple, lavender, pink and white.

Siberian flag iris
Iris sibirica

An adaptable and trouble-free iris ideally suited to sunny sites in moist, fertile soil. The small, neat flowers are a rich purple-blue, with darkly veined white throats. Two to three are held on each stem above upright grassy leaves in summer. This species is not invasive and will also grow in drier, slightly shadier conditions.

▲ Japanese iris

HEIGHT 90 cm (3 ft). **SPREAD** 45 cm (18 in). ◯
ALTERNATIVES *I. s.* **'Perry's Blue'** has heavily veined china-blue flowers. *I. s.* **'White Swirl'** has white flowers with yellow veins.

Ligularia dentata

A handsome and impressive flowering and foliage plant for late summer colour, *L. dentata* produces clusters of large orange-yellow daisy-like flowers on branching stems from midsummer to early autumn. The large, heart-shaped leaves are grey green and form broad but compact clumps.
HEIGHT 90–120 cm (3–4 ft). **SPREAD** 60–90 cm (2–3 ft). ⬤
ALTERNATIVES *L. d.* **'Desdemona'** has very attractive purplish-bronze leaves that provide a striking colour combination with the orange-yellow flowers. *L.* **'Gregynog Gold'** is a hybrid with richly veined green leaves and flowers borne on large pyramidal spikes.

Ligularia stenocephala

This species is a stately, spectacular flowering and foliage plant for rich, moist soils. Towering spires of starry yellow flowers appear on tall, purplish stems from mid to late summer. The deep green, rounded leaves have toothed edges and form large, loose clumps beneath the flower spikes.

HEIGHT 1.2–1.8 m (4–6 ft). **SPREAD** 60–90 cm (2–3 ft). ⬤
ALTERNATIVES *L.* **'The Rocket'** is an especially good form with black stems and jagged leaves. *L. przewalskii* is a similar species with more deeply lobed leaves and dark purple-green stems.

Cardinal flower
Lobelia cardinalis

Cardinal flower is a vivid, late-flowering perennial for rich, moist soils and although it is not completely hardy the tall spikes of bright scarlet flowers late in the summer make it worth growing. The glossy, lance-shaped leaves can be bright green or purple-bronze. Mulch in autumn to protect from frosts.
HEIGHT 75–90 cm (2½–3 ft). **SPREAD** 30–45 cm (12–18 in). ◯ ⬤ Frost hardy to –5°C (23°F).
ALTERNATIVES *L.* **'Queen Victoria'** is the best scarlet-flowered hybrid with red-purple foliage. *L.* × *gerardii* **'Vedrariensis'** is a hardier hybrid with violet-purple flowers and dark green oval leaves tinged red.

Creeping jenny
Lysimachia nummularia

A vigorous carpeting perennial plant, this species is extremely useful for covering

damp banks and concealing pond edges. Small evergreen leaves are held on long rooting stems which can be invasive in damp or drier conditions. Bright yellow flowers appear in summer.
HEIGHT 2.5–5 cm (1–2 in). **SPREAD** 75–90 cm (2½–3 ft). ◯ ⬤
ALTERNATIVES *L. n.* **'Aurea'** is a less vigorous variety with attractive, soft yellow leaves. *L. punctata* (**large yellow loosestrife**) is another vigorous species with yellow flowers on upright stems (to 90 cm/3ft).

Purple loosestrife
Lythrum salicaria

A long-flowering, desirable perennial for the waterside or bog garden. Slender, upright spikes of purple-pink flowers appear from midsummer to early autumn. Small, lance-shaped leaves are borne beneath on the flower stems. Damp or wet soils and a little shade are preferable.
HEIGHT 75–90 cm (2½–3 ft). **SPREAD** 45–60 cm (18–24 in). ◯ ⬤
ALTERNATIVES *L. s.* **'Feuerkerze'** has rose-red flowers. *L. s.* **'Robert'** is a compact variety with clear pink flowers. *L. virgatum* **'The Rocket'** is a similar species with deep pink flowers.

▼ *Ligularia przewalskii*

117

▶ Bistort or knotweed

Shuttlecock/ostrich feather fern
Matteuccia struthiopteris
A beautiful and striking fresh green fern for deep, moisture-retentive soils and shade. The graceful upright fronds are lance-shaped and arranged symmetrically like shuttlecock feathers. They are freshest and most delicate when unfurling in spring, becoming yellow in the autumn. The central dark brown fertile fronds remain erect and decorative over winter.
HEIGHT 1 m (3$^1/_4$ ft). **SPREAD** 45 cm (18 in).
◐ ●

Yellow musk
Mimulus luteus
A spreading, groundcovering perennial for wet soils, bog gardens and larger wildlife ponds. Bright yellow snapdragon-like flowers, often spotted red-brown, appear in long succession throughout summer. The hairy mid-green leaves create lush cover, making it useful for disguising pond edges.

▼ *Shuttlecock or ostrich feather fern*

It will also grow in shallow water.
HEIGHT 30–45 cm (12–18 in). **SPREAD** 45 cm (18 in). ○ ◐
ALTERNATIVES *M. l.* **'Variegatus'** has green and white variegated leaves. *M. l.* **hose-in-hose** is a curious double variety with one flower tube inside the other.

Royal fern
Osmunda regalis
A magnificent specimen fern ideal for the water's edge or shallow margins of larger ponds. The large divided fronds are a bright mid green becoming yellow-brown in autumn. Mature plants bear tall rust-brown fertile fronds. This fern requires lime-free soil.
HEIGHT 1.2–1.8 m (4–6 ft). **SPREAD** 1.2–1.8 m (4–6 ft). ○ ◐

Bistort/knotweed
Persicaria bistorta 'Superba'
This vigorous perennial looks best when massed in damp ground close to large water features. Soft pink bottlebrush-like flowers are produced throughout the summer on erect stems above broad, groundcovering foliage.
HEIGHT 60–75 cm (2–2$^1/_2$ ft). **SPREAD** 60–90 cm (2–3 ft). ○ ◐

Candlelabra primula
Primula SPECIES AND VARIETIES
These primulas make elegant and colourful flowering perennials for mass planting in a bog garden or at the side of a pool or stream. Whorls of primrose-like flowers in a vast range of colours are held on erect stems above the foliage in early summer. The lush clumps of pale green lance-shaped leaves make good groundcover. Dappled shade and rich, moist, slightly acidic soils are the most suitable conditions.
HEIGHT 60–75 cm (2–2$^1/_2$ ft). **SPREAD** 30–45 cm (12–18 in). ◐
P. **aurantiaca** has orange-red flowers; *P.* **beesiana** has rose-purple flowers with yellow eyes and those of *P.* **bulleyana** are vivid orange. *P.* **japonica** is a slightly smaller species with deep red flowers. *P. j.* **'Postford White'** has white flowers with yellow eyes. *P.* **prolifera** is a vigorous species with golden-yellow flowers. *P.* **pulverulenta** has claret red flowers with purple eyes. *P. p.* **'Bartley Pink'** is an excellent variety with soft pink flowers.

Drumstick primula
Primula denticulata
Drumstick primulas are vigorous perennials for early spring colour in partial shade and

moist, slightly acidic soils. Dense globular clusters of pale lavender flowers appear on short stems just as the leaves develop In spring. The grey-green lance-shaped leaves eventually knit together to form neat weed-suppressing clumps of foliage.

HEIGHT 30–45 cm (12–18 in). **SPREAD** 30–45 cm (12–18 in).

ALTERNATIVE *P. d.* **var.** *alba* has white flowers.

Giant Himalayan cowslip
Primula florindae
One of the most vigorous and beautiful of the waterside primulas for mass planting, this species has pendulous bell-shaped yellow flowers. They are sweetly scented and are held on tall stems in summer. Some selections have copper or apricot-tinted flowers. In rich, damp and slightly acidic soils the broad lance-shaped leaves will be dense enough to suppress most weeds.

HEIGHT 90–120 cm (3–4 ft). **SPREAD** 30–60 cm (12–24 in).

◀ **Candelabra primulas**

Ornamental rhubarb
Rheum palmatum
This impressive foliage plant is used as a specimen by the pool and as a substitute for *Gunnera* in smaller gardens. In rich, damp soils the large, deeply cut leaves can be up to 75 cm (2¹/₂ ft) long and wide, forming huge, weed-suppressing clumps. Tall shafts of fluffy creamy-white flower panicles are sent up on stout stems in early summer.

HEIGHT 1.5–2.4 m (5–8ft). **SPREAD** 1.8–2.1 m (6–7 ft).

ALTERNATIVES *R. p.* **'Atrosanguineum'** is a striking cultivar producing crimson flowers and olive-green foliage with red-purple undersides. *R.* **'Ace of Hearts'** is a dwarf form (60–90 cm/2–3 ft) with pale pink flowers and dark heart-shaped leaves tinted crimson on the reverse.

Rodgersia
Rodgersia **SPECIES AND VARIETIES**
A group of magnificent architectural foliage plants for the bog or woodland water garden, rodgersias have large green jagged or deeply lobed leaves which are often tinged bronze. Panicles of pink or creamy-white flowers are borne above the foliage in summer. Ideal conditions are deep, moist fertile soils with some shade and shelter.

HEIGHT 90–120 cm (3–4 ft). **SPREAD** 90 cm (3 ft).

R. **aesculifolia** has large horse chestnut-shaped leaves and white flowers. *R.* **pinnata** **'Superba'** has bronze-green, divided leaves and pink flowers. The foliage of *R.* **podophylla** is broadly jagged and bronze; the flowers are creamy white. *R.* **sambucifolia** has green elder-like leaves and white flowers. *R.* **tabularis** (recently renamed *Astilboides tabularis*) also has white flowers but large green parasol-like leaves.

Variegated prairie cord grass
Spartina pectinata 'Aureomarginata'
A vigorous, arching grass that grows best in moist soils near water. The long, ribbon-like

▲ *Rodgersia podophylla*

green leaves are margined gold-yellow and turn to brown in autumn and winter. Graceful stems of red-brown flower spikes appear above the foliage from late summer.

HEIGHT 1.5–1.8 m (5–6 ft). **SPREAD** indefinite.

Globe flower
Trollius europaeus
Globe flower is a cheerful and compact spring-flowering perennial for moist soils. Single, rounded and many-petalled lemon-yellow flowers appear in late spring above deeply divided mid-green leaves. It will flower more freely and make denser groundcover in heavy, loamy soils that stay moist during warm weather.

HEIGHT 60 cm (2 ft). **SPREAD** 45 cm (18 in).

ALTERNATIVES *T. e.* **'Superbus'** has incurving petals, making the flower even more globe-like. *T.* × *cultorum* **'Orange Princess'** is a slightly taller hybrid with orange-gold flowers. *T.* **pumilus** is a dwarf species (15 cm/6 in) with more open yellow flowers.

WATERSIDE PLANTS

These can be defined as the permanent structure plants such as trees and shrubs that provide a backdrop or context for the pond. Some will create shelter and enclosure while others will stand alone as feature plants, reflecting in the water and evoking a certain mood or atmosphere. Because they are large plants that will make an immediate as well as lasting impact, they need to be chosen and sited with care. Many, for example willows and bamboos, prefer moist soils but beware of invasive roots – some species of bamboo can pierce pond liners, so clump-forming varieties should be chosen in association with ponds.

Japanese maple
Acer palmatum VARIETIES
These beautiful foliage shrubs can become small multi-stemmed trees over time. The delicate palmate leaves hang gracefully from layered branches and are green, purple or soft yellow with fiery orange-red autumn colours. Small, hanging clusters of purple-red flowers appear in spring. Japanese maples look stunning as feature shrubs near to and reflected in water and create a strong oriental look in a garden. Neutral to acidic soils which remain cool and moist are ideal. Light dappled shade and shelter from cold winds and spring frosts are essential if the soft foliage is not to be damaged.
HEIGHT 4.5 m (15 ft) over time. SPREAD 4.5 m (15 ft) over time.
A. p. **'Bloodgood'** is an excellent purple-leaved variety with brilliant red autumn colours. *A. p.* **var.** *dissectum* is a smaller variety (to 2.4 m/8 ft) with deeply dissected bright green leaves that turn bronze-yellow in autumn. *A. p.* **'Dissectum Atropurpureum'** has small, deeply dissected purple leaves with orange-red autumn colours.

Red-stemmed dogwood
Cornus alba VARIETIES
Vigorous background shrubs grown primarily

▲ Japanese maple 'Dissectum Atropurpureum'

for their winter stem colour, these dogwoods have dark green oval leaves that become orange or plum-red in autumn and fall to expose the red stems. To retain the winter colour and keep the plant within bounds the stems must be cut back almost to ground level each spring. Clusters of white flowers appear in late spring only on plants that have not been cut back. In larger gardens varieties with different-coloured stems can be mass planted together with stunning results. Moisture-retentive soils are the most suitable, although dogwoods will tolerate both dry and waterlogged soils.
HEIGHT 1.8–2.4 m (6–8 ft). SPREAD 1.8–2.4 m (6–8 ft).
C. a. **'Aurea'** has soft yellow leaves and red stems and requires part shade. *C. a.* **'Kesselringii'** has purple green leaves and almost black stems. *C. a.* **'Elegantissima'** produces green and white variegated leaves and has red stems. *C. a.* **'Sibirica'** has the brightest crimson-red stems; *C.* **stolonifera** **'Flaviramea'** is a similar species with bright green-yellow stems.

Bamboo
Fargesia nitida
An impressive clump-forming bamboo for screening or specimen planting, this species had dark purple upright canes that are densely packed and arch outwards as they

age. Each cane produces masses of small, narrow evergreen leaves. Moist soils with some shade and shelter produce the lushest foliage. Bamboos are exotic foliage plants which can be used to great effect in oriental and subtropical schemes.
HEIGHT 4.5–6 m (15–20 ft). SPREAD 1.5–1.8 cm (5–6 ft).
ALTERNATIVE *F. murielae* (umbrella bamboo) is a slightly smaller (3–4.5 m/10–15 ft) and more tolerant species with green-yellow canes that arch further outwards.

Silver banner grass
Miscanthus sacchariflorus
This imposing grass with luxuriant foliage creates a tropical effect around the water garden. The broad, arching green leaves have a silver midrib and hang from upright stems, creating stout bamboo-like clumps. In hot years white flower plumes appear in autumn and last through the winter. Deep, rich soils that do not dry out in summer are ideal. Although a vigorous, spreading plant, it is useful for background planting and creating screening and shelter.
HEIGHT 2.7–3 m (9–10 ft). SPREAD indefinite.

Maiden grass
Miscanthus sinensis 'Gracillimus'
An elegant fine-leaved grass for mass or accent planting around the water garden, maiden grass has tall, upright, slender grey-green leaves that arch outwards at the tips, creating a neat vase-shaped clump. The foliage turns bronze in autumn, when silky white flower plumes may appear. Newer hybrids are more reliably flowering, continuing to look impressive over winter. Moist soils which do not become too dry in summer are ideal.
HEIGHT 1.2–1.5 cm (4–5ft). SPREAD 60–90 cm (2–3 ft).
ALTERNATIVES *M. s.* **'Morning Light'** is a beautiful variety with fine foliage variegated white. *M. s.* **'Zebrinus'** (**zebra grass**) is a distinctive specimen grass with wider green leaves banded yellow and pinkish-brown fan-shaped flower plumes.

New Zealand flax
Phormium CULTIVARS

Dramatic evergreen foliage plants used singly or en masse and creating a sub-tropical effect. The upright sword-shaped leaves are either rigid or more lax and come in a variety of colours. Tall spikes of bronze-red flowers appear in summer on mature plants. Phormiums are slightly tender and prefer warm, sheltered sites and moist but open soils. They also look good in containers.

HEIGHT 1.5–1.8 m (5–6 ft). SPREAD 90–120 cm (3–4 ft). ◯ ◉ Frost hardy to –10°C (14°F).
ALTERNATIVES *P. tenax* **'Purpureum'** is a taller variety with bronze-purple leaves. *P.* **'Sundowner'** has erect copper-red leaves with pink and cream margins. *P.* **'Yellow Wave'** is more lax with bright yellow variegated leaves. *P.* **'Bronze Baby'** is a dwarf form (to 90 cm/3 ft) with bronze-red foliage. *P. cookianum* × *hookeri* **'Cream Delight'** is a smaller (to 1.5 m/5 ft) species with lax green leaves striped creamy yellow.

Fishpole/golden bamboo
Phyllostachys aurea

A tall clump-forming specimen bamboo for a sunny border but also looking good in a container, this plant has stiff, upright bright green canes that fade to creamy yellow in full sun. The evergreen leaves are long and narrow. It will tolerate drier conditions.
HEIGHT 3–4.5 m (10–15 ft). SPREAD 1.2–1.5 m (4–5 ft). ◯
ALTERNATIVE *P. nigra* (**black bamboo**) is a similar species which develops glossy black canes over time. It requires some shelter.

Pleioblastus viridistriatus

This is a lower growing variegated bamboo that slowly spreads to form an attractive and effective groundcover. The purplish stems support large vivid yellow and green striped leaves. Although it is evergreen, the spring foliage will be freshest if the leaves are cut down in autumn.
HEIGHT 1.2–1.5 m (4–5 ft). SPREAD indefinite. ◯ ◉
ALTERNATIVE *P. variegatus* is a slightly smaller (60–120 cm/2–4 ft) species with green and white striped foliage.

Scarlet willow
Salix alba var. *vitellina* 'Britzensis'

A form of the white willow grown primarily for its bright orange-scarlet winter stems. To maintain it as a shrub and to produce the

▲ *Pleioblastus viridistriatus*

brightest young stems the plant must be cut back nearly to ground level annually or biennially in spring. Alternatively it can be grown as a tree and pollarded (pruned back to a crown above the main stem at about 1.2–1.5 m/4–5 ft above ground level). Unpruned shrubs produce small yellow male catkins in mid-spring before the narrow grey-green leaves. They will eventually form large, upright, wind-resistant trees. Damp soils produce the best specimens.
HEIGHT and SPREAD are dependent on pruning regime. ◯ ◉
ALTERNATIVE *S. a.* var. *vitellina* (**golden willow**) has bright golden-yellow stems.

Golden weeping willow
Salix × *sepulcralis* var. *chrysocoma*

A fast-growing and wide-spreading dome-shaped tree, evocative of the waterside but for large gardens only. Slender yellow-green leaves hang from golden-yellow pendulous branches, creating beautiful curtains of greenery. In winter the bright stems are particularly decorative. It is often planted beside water but will grow in any moisture-retentive soil.
HEIGHT 15–18 m (50–60 ft). SPREAD 10–15 m (33–50 ft). ◯

◀ **Maiden grass**

8 • Fish Selector

A healthy pond will soon attract a large amount of wildlife both to the water and the area around it. Insects, amphibians and birds will all appear without further encouragement from the gardener, along with myriad different microscopic life forms. The exception to this spontaneous arrival of living creatures is, of course, fish, which you will have to introduce to the pond yourself.

On the following pages you will find a selection of fish listed according to their suitability for large, medium and small-sized ponds and water features, including native species for wildlife ponds. To help you keep your fish in prime condition there is also advice on population numbers and maintaining water quality as well as a list of pests, diseases and predators to look out for.

FISH IN PONDS

When you are buying fish do not be too shy to ask advice from your supplier, but use your own common sense too. Look at the fish in the bag before you take it home. Its colour should be good and all its fins should be held high and proud rather than clamped to the body. Examine the fish all over for any marks, missing scales or pale spots or patches. A covering of slime, a paler colour and abnormally visible blood vessels are all signs of an unhealthy fish. Look at its eyes, too; warning signs are swelling, redness, or eyes that don't match. If the fish fails any test, reject it.

A matter of balance

To keep fish successfully your pond must be balanced. This means that all the wastes produced by fish or other creatures must be broken down safely. There is more than one way to achieve this.

If your pond is well planted and stocked quite lightly with fish, the plants will break down the wastes the fish produce and rainwater, as it falls into the pond, will dilute them further. This natural balance can be supplemented by replacing up to 50 per cent of the water on a regular basis, which alone will safely dilute wastes in any type of pond.

However, most gardeners rely on a filter for their pond. Filters take advantage of a natural phenomenon called denitrification by offering the best conditions for the bacteria that promote the process, which requires the conversion of ammonia to nitrates.

▲ Koi are greedy and demand high-quality filtration

The ammonia cycle

When fish excrete and respire, and when anything organic dies and breaks down in your pond, ammonia is produced. Ammonia is toxic to fish in sufficient concentrations, but can be broken down by bacteria that are present in every pond. These aerobic *Nitrosomonas* bacteria use up oxygen as they convert the ammonia to nitrite – which is, if anything, even more toxic to your fish. Another type of aerobic bacteria called *Nitrobacter* then continue the process, converting nitrite to nitrate, which is a plant (and algae) food and far less damaging to the fish in the pond.

Finally, in some circumstances, nitrates are broken down to nitrogen gas by anaerobic bacteria – those not requiring oxygen. This gas disperses throughout the surface of the pond.

These helpful bacteria are sessile, which means that they attach themselves permanently to surfaces. A well-designed, well-maintained filter provides an ideal home for these bacteria. It offers somewhere comfortable to live, with a constant flow of well-oxygenated water, and the all-important supply of adequate amounts of ammonia and nitrites to convert.

You can buy solutions and impregnated pads containing these bacteria, but they will appear spontaneously in your pond and will build up naturally if it is well run.

▲ A filter unit with UV clarifier on top

The filter system

To run your filter you will require a pump in the pond to feed the water into it. The full volume of the pond should be pumped through the filter once per hour. Many fishkeepers prefer to use a pump that also pumps small solids into the filter too. Collected in there, rather than on the base of the pond, they are easier to remove.

If solids are to be collected in a filter it is a good idea to choose or build a filter with a vortex, brushes or some other sort of pre-filter to collect them before they clog the filter media where the bacteria live. Pre-filter sponges and brushes should be cleaned regularly in a bucket or other container of pond water (not under the tap, which may kill helpful bacteria on the pre-filter).

▲ An advanced commercial filter unit incorporating a solids-removing pre-filter, brushes and sponges

Filters vary so much in design that it is not practical to offer general advice about them here. Your dealer will be the best starting point for information, based on the number of fish you want to stock, the size of the pond and possibly also what planting it contains.

Other items

Most fishkeepers choose to buy an ultra-violet clarifier for their pond. By pumping water through one of these, the pond owner can ensure that green water algae are disrupted, clumped together and, if there is an efficient filter, removed. They must always be used in conjunction with a filter and many manufacturers now guarantee clear water if they are used properly.

Many fishkeepers also keep a large air pump handy. This allows them to pump extra air into their ponds and filters on warm, still days and, for example, when medications or anti-algae chemical treatments have been used.

Most air pumps will need to be protected from the weather and require large airstones or other air diffusers and long lengths of airline, both of which usually need to be purchased separately.

New ponds and overstocking

The main problem that arises when the owner of a pond stocks it with fish for the first time is the production of more wastes than the filter can cope with. This is the result of introducing too many fish too quickly and feeding them too much. This 'new pond syndrome' can be avoided by stocking only one large fish or four small ones at a time. Take advice from your supplier, quoting the size of your pond, the existing stock and the size of the fish you wish to buy.

Predators

Certain fish are too predatory to keep in your pond, but unfortunately there are outside predators too. While these may be welcome at a wildlife pond they can be problematic at a pond stocked with large fish.

HOW MANY FISH?

To find out how many fish you can safely build up to, measure the length and width of the pond (rounding down where the shape is irregular) in centimetres (inches), multiply one by the other and divide by 120 (48). This gives you a rough guide as to the total number of centimetres (inches) of fish, minus their tails, you can keep in your pond.

In Britain herons are the major problem. A protected and unusually intelligent species, they are growing in confidence. A net is the only guaranteed solution and even then it should be suspended well above the surface of the pond.

Further predators include other birds, domestic cats, foxes, escaped mink and snakes – the latter even in the UK, where there are so few species. Grass snakes swim well and do like a fish supper.

Again, most of these can be deterred by a net set well above the surface of the pond (though snakes are the exception here) and by other methods such as heavy pondside planting, raised sides to the pond and a lowered water level, fishing nylon strung around and across the pond and even cables producing a mild electric shock. Most of these are available commercially.

▼ Raised ponds edges may deter predators

FISH FOR LARGE PONDS
(more than 6825 litres/1500 gal)

CARP
Koi
Cyprinus carpio

As koi is the Japanese word for 'carp' it is incorrect to refer to these fish as koi carp, though many people do so. Nishikigoi, the full name, means 'brocaded carp', a reference to the many colours that the fish appear in. Combinations of white, orange (technically called red), black and brown can produce a wide range of hues.

There are also different scale markings. The main types are metallic (gin rin) and large-scaled (doitsu or German), where the scales are arranged in a line down the spine of the fish from head to tail.

Koi are friendly and beautiful fish and quite hardy, which might make them seem ideal for the average water garden. However, they grow large (potentially very large indeed) and are very greedy, so they demand three things for total success: deep water (a minimum of 1.2 m/4 ft depth over a considerable area of the pond); a large pond of at least 6825 litres (1500 gal) for a small number of fish, and high-quality filtration to cope with their wastes. Consequently, they are not for the unfiltered pond or for gardeners who want a splash of colour in their pond but are not interested in cleaning

▲ Small koi in a correctly maintained environment will quickly reach 30 cm (12 in)

out and maintaining an extensive filter system, providing a regular food supply and checking their fish carefully each day.

The best koi are also expensive to buy, particularly those from Japan. Some experts feel the latter are the only worthwhile koi, but cheaper fish from other countries, especially Israel and Malaysia, will still look lovely, even if they do not satisfy the purist. If you want to keep the best high-priced fish, specialize in them alone and build your pond accordingly.
SIZE GUIDE Koi can reach 60 cm (2 ft) in length and in the case of some varieties (chagoi, for example) are far larger.

Ghost carp
Cyprinus carpio

Ghost carp are a cross between koi and mirror carp, producing a silver-grey fish with a skull-like marking on the head – hence the rather fanciful name. A few ghost carp with tinges of pale red are also now available.

◀ Mirror carp are hard to see in a pond

▶ This koi is a brood fish from a British koi breeding venture. Koi are now bred world-wide, but the best are still Japanese

Ghost carp traditionally eat like an aquatic horse, and are tough as a mule – but, like koi, they need a large pond and like-minded companions as they can be greedy and boisterous.

SIZE GUIDE Ghost carp reach similar sizes to koi.

Mirror carp
Cyprinus carpio
Mirror carp are a hardy, naturally occurring variety of common carp where some scales are overly large. On doitsu koi (and the 'German carp') these have been line-bred into a neat row along the back, but they can appear randomly all over the sides of the fish.

Such fish are lovely when viewed side on, but because of their natural colouring they are hard to see in a large pond. A cheap shusui koi which has a grey/white doitsu band of scales on its back over a red body is a better choice as it will be much easier to see and will also come to the surface more frequently.

SIZE GUIDE Mirror carp can also reach 60 cm (2 ft) or more.

Grass carp
Ctenopharyngodon idella
These fish have sometimes been touted as the cure for all weed problems, including blanket weed. This might make them very attractive to the water gardener who has a vision of a weed-free pond, but unfortunately it is only a dream. In a well-fed pond, grass carp will eat pellets and ignore stringy blanket weed; in a well-planted pond they may well prefer other plants to the filamentous algae.

Again this is a naturally coloured fish, so it will not be easy to see (unless you buy the gold or semi-albino versions). Another disadvantage is that it has a habit of jumping out of ponds. In the UK a licence is now attached to its import and sale.

SIZE GUIDE Grass carp can match the lengths of other carp but are less deep-bodied than koi.

You may also see for sale
The fully scaled dark-bodied **common carp**, grand-daddy of ghost and mirror carp and koi, and the **leather carp** – a scaleless (or near scaleless) version of the common carp. Both belong to the species *Cyprinus carpio*.

GOLDFISH
Common goldfish
Carrassius auratus
The common goldfish is an excellent choice in both large and smaller ponds. Its oxygen demands and need for space are low compared to other pond species, and it will survive a degree of pollution (though that does not mean it will enjoy it.)

The common goldfish can be found in shades between orange – the 'gold' that gives the fish its name – and red, as well as white, black, bronze and yellow and combinations of all those hues. Colours in goldfish are rarely very fixed; they can change as the fish ages, sometimes apparently overnight.

Goldfish can be long-lived – a lifespan of 10 or more years is not uncommon. They thrive if stocked in sensible numbers in a well-planted pond requiring no filtration and often little feeding.

SIZE GUIDE Common goldfish may reach 30 cm (12 in) in length in a large pond.

Comets
Carrassius auratus
Comets are generally gold (orange) or a

▲ **Comets are a variety of common goldfish well suited to large ponds**

combination of white and red, and can be distinguished by a long flowing tail (caudal fin) and a long thin body, nowhere near as deep as common goldfish. They are perhaps better suited to a larger pond as they tend to grow bigger than other goldfish.

SIZE GUIDE Comets can grow to a length of 45 cm (18 in).

Shubunkins
Carrassius auratus
Shubunkins sport speckles of black and

◀ **The common goldfish is the ideal pond fish**

▲ Shubunkins have a distinctive calico pattern

▲ Note the deeper body and twin tails of this fancy goldfish

'nacreous' (metallic) scales over a red and white or mainly red base colour, the whole effect sometimes being called 'calico'. It is reputed to be one of the hardiest of the goldfish varieties.

You may see Bristol or London shubunkins on sale at specialist dealers. They are mainly differentiated by the shape and size of the tail, which should be larger than a common goldfish but shorter and wider than a comet.

The vast majority of imported shubunkins today are not of good-quality pattern and colour. However, they are still hardy and so a useful addition to a pond.

SIZE GUIDE A huge shubunkin may grow to 30 cm (12 in).

Crucian carp
Carrassius carrassius
This species is the ancestor of all goldfish. Crucians are tubby natural bronze-coloured fish that will be difficult to see individually, but they are hardy and happy in shoals of crucians or with other goldfish.

SIZE GUIDE A very large crucian may reach 60 cm (2 ft).

▶ **The golden rudd is an attractive colour sport of the true species**

You may also see for sale
Fancy goldfish
This loose term covers all the twin tail and other fancy varieties, such as orandas, lionheads, blackmoors and more extreme varieties such as celestials and bubble eyes.

These can be stocked in ponds in temperate climates from June to early October with few ill effects as long as you avoid the very extreme varieties (such as the bubble-eyes) in favour of the tougher ones such as moors or orandas. Make sure that there are no tail-nibbling or exceptionally greedy or boisterous species in the pond with them, or they may starve.

Some pond owners in temperate climates leave fancy goldfish outdoors all year – and one British breeder in the south of England keeps all his fancy goldfish stock outdoors over winter in quite shallow ponds.

BLUE OR GOLDEN ORFE
Idus idus
The orfe reached its height of popularity in the UK in the 1970s, when many people bred them. As they can be colourful and swim near the surface they are definitely ornamental. However, their surface habit is partly because of their high oxygen demand; they are skittish and jump a lot in pursuit of flies, often ending up on the ground outside the pool; and they react badly to some medications, a common problem being a bent body or tail – something often seen even in aquatic shops.

Their body shape is more built for speed than other, portlier, species, but because they lie just below the surface they are still a tempting and relatively easy target for predators. They should certainly not be kept in a pond without some surface or marginal

▲ **Golden orfe**

plant cover, and you will need to have a large air pump handy to oxygenate the pond on hot, still nights.

SIZE GUIDE Orfe can grow to a length of 60 cm (2 ft) or more.

RUDD
Scardinius erythropthalmus
Rudd are available in gold and orange as well as the natural olive-brown with bright red fins, although even rudd that have been line-bred to bring out red or orange coloration seem to retain much of their natural colouring under the brighter hues. The red fins make them an attractive fish in any form. However, rudd do share many of the disadvantages of orfe, including sensitivity to some medication.

SIZE GUIDE Rudd in a pond reach no more than 30 cm (12 in), although larger specimens are found in the wild.

TENCH
Tinca tinca
Many pond owners are sold tench with the promise that they will clear up food that sinks to the base of the pond. In fact, there is no such thing as a scavenger fish – although it seems many people want to buy one. Nothing that swims will hoover up rotting food from the base of a pond and

miraculously convert it to pure water. All living creatures excrete.

Tench are lovely peaceable fish, but even though colourful ornamental varieties are available you will rarely be able to see them in your pond. They are among the species that hug the bottom most closely and are naturally dark olive brown or even black. They hibernate given the chance, so prefer a deep, undisturbed pond. If you can see them the pond is probably too shallow.

Far from relying on them to clean up leftovers, you may need to feed them sinking pellets – and you will never know if the food is eaten.

SIZE GUIDE Tench can reach 60 cm (2 ft) in a pond, but usually stay smaller.

FISH FOR MEDIUM PONDS
(2275–6825 litres/500–1500 gal)

FAT HEAD MINNOW
(also called **rosy red** or **golden minnow**)
Pimephales promelas
This is an American species that can cope well with pond life all year round. They closely resemble a European minnow (see page 129) in shape and, when seen in their natural form, colour too. But the Xanthic golden version is sold as an ornamental, and the lifestyle of this whole minnow family, natural or gold, is very different to the European species. Fish on sale in the UK will probably have been bred in Britain or the Far East.

These are easy, keen surface feeders that spawn securely in 'caves' (the males

watching over the eggs and fry) in folds of your liner, in the gaps in planting baskets, or under lily pads. Always stock a shoal of six or more.

SIZE GUIDE The largest size this species will reach will probably be no more than 10 cm (4 in) long.

You can also stock
The following species suggested for large ponds will also cope well with life in a small to medium pond:

Ghost carp (see page 124), but probably only one at a time.

Goldfish: Common goldfish, shubunkins, crucian carp and comets (see pages 125–6), although the latter do best in larger ponds. At certain times of the year goldfish can have predatory tendencies – mainly before and after spawning in the early summer – and larger goldfish may eat smaller minnows or their fry. On the whole, though, they will live together amicably.

Tench (see left).

BITTERLING
Rhodeus sericeus
These little fish are found throughout most of Europe but are not endemic to the UK and now require a licence before they can be sold. This is a pity, as they would be ideal for a small or medium pond and are interesting for their strange behaviour of laying eggs inside a mussel.

▼ **Golden minnow**

FISH FOR SMALL PONDS
(less than 2275 litres/500 gal)

If you do not mind keeping an aquarium handy for the winter months, there are several species that will cope with rising temperatures in a small pond from late May to late September. However, even the hardiest of these must be brought in before the water sinks much below 10°C (50°F).

WHITE CLOUD MOUNTAIN MINNOW

Tanichthys albonubes
The White Cloud Mountain minnow, a Chinese species, will do well in a pond in summer and may spawn. Problems will arise when you want to remove them in the autumn. They are small and hide in plants; you may also have to find shoals of tiny fry.

Always stock at least six – they are inexpensive, so buying two dozen or more is not out of the question. You will then see the courting displays of the males, with tiny fins held proudly high. They are quite colourful, though seen from above the back is dark. They are very hardy and will thrive at temperatures from 16°C (61°F) to 26°C (79°F).
SIZE GUIDE They rarely reach 5 cm (2 in).

ROSY BARB

Barbus conchonius
The rosy barb is not unlike a small goldfish in

◀ Long-finned rosy barb

appearance and is in fact distantly related to that species, although much smaller in size.

Rosy barbs originate from Bengal, India, but are quite happy at temperatures below 21°C (70°F) and might find some tropical tanks a little too warm. They like probing around in a silty substrate – something they can do outdoors – and are best kept in a small, well-planted pond.

The males darken in colour when spawning (which they happily do all summer outdoors), which adds to their attractive appearance. A long-finned variety is available but it is less suitable for ponds because the fins are easily damaged and any injury is more difficult to spot than when they are kept in a tank.
SIZE GUIDE Rosy barbs reach no more than 10 cm (5 in) in length.

PARADISE FISH

Macropodus opercualris
There is more than one species with the common name of paradise fish, but this species is the fish to buy.

Legendarily hardy, and comfortable at water temperatures as low as 10°C (50°F), the paradise fish has beautiful blue and orange colouring. It is an anabantoid, which means that not only does it have gills but it is also able to breathe atmospheric air at the surface of the water via a special organ located in its head.

◀ **White Cloud Mountain minnow**

The only drawback is their aggression. You can probably keep only a pair and they must be in a pond with hiding places for the female. If you are very lucky, the male will build a bubble nest at the surface and the pair will spawn.

▲ **Paradise fish**

OTHER CHOICES

This is not an exhaustive list of suitable species, and there are many more possibilities. Look out for *Gambusia* sp., the zebra danio (*Brachydanio rerio*), and some of the plecs (suckermouth catfish). However, always read up about the fish and take advice before experimenting. It is essential to bring them into a warm house or outhouse when winter comes. Finally, never release any fish, native or alien, into local natural waters.

Many owners of wildlife ponds believe that fish have no place in their pond. Most of the ornamental species kept in the UK originally come from overseas and are therefore not a part of British wildlife. The exception is the crucian carp, which is a native of the UK.

There is also the drawback that larger fish eat the young of rarer creatures such as frogs and newts. However, there are several smaller species of fish which will keep mosquitoes at bay but will not do much damage to anything larger.

Though small, they will require the deeper water needed by larger fish. They probably will not need filtration and, because they are native species, they may breed in the pond and keep up their numbers. However, they will be easy targets for almost every predator that can visit the pond, including some insect predators such as great diving beetles and the larvae of dragonflies (see page 131).

EUROPEAN MINNOW
Phoxinus phoxinus
These subtly coloured fish are always on the move and must be kept in shoals. They are not really suitable for ponds that get very warm in summer (mainly shallow ones which quickly overheat) as, although they are occasionally found in still waters, the European minnow is a river species. They may need extra aeration in summer, which may damage the 'natural wildlife' appearance of the pond. European minnows should not be collected from rivers but purchased from dealers who specialize in cold-water species. They spawn between late May and July.

This species will probably do well in medium to larger-sized ponds – if they escape being eaten.
SIZE GUIDE A very large minnow may reach 10 cm (4 in).

◀ A wildlife pond provides an ideal habitat for many species of insects and amphibians such as frogs

STICKLEBACKS
Gasterosteus aculeatus
There are several species of stickleback found all over Europe and the adaptable three-spined variety, which is very common in Britain, even lives in brackish water and in the sea. They are an ideal addition to a wildlife pond.

Their bodies are covered with bony plates with a silver sheen, making them look almost prehistoric, and the spines are so tough that they are capable of being mouthed by a large predator fish before being rejected intact.

◀ European minnows will do well in a large, deep wildlife pond

▶ Sticklebacks make fascinating inhabitants for a small pond

Sticklebacks are worth keeping simply to observe their spawning behaviour, as the males build a nest in their weedy territory and try to defend it against all comers. They do not always succeed – it is not unknown for trout to acquire the habit of swallowing the whole nest for the eggs inside.

The males have a bright purplish-red breast at this time; there is no mistaking a pregnant female either, as full of eggs, they look as though their lower body has been stuffed with cotton wool from tail to thorax. **SIZE GUIDE** A very big stickleback may reach 7 cm (3 in).

GUDGEON
Gobio gobio
Like the stickleback, the gudgeon is a species found in European rivers. A whiskery

▶ **Gudgeon need well-oxygenated water**

bottom-dweller which might be mistaken for a catfish, it rarely reaches 12 cm (5 in) in length and is very slim, apparently making it an excellent candidate for small ponds. However, even though gudgeon thrive in many still waters, especially in worked-out gravel pits near rivers, they are really fish from well-oxygenated streams and the

minimum requirement is life in a relatively cool larger pond. They are an ideal choice for anyone who is fortunate enough to have a deepish artificial stream built into their pond. Gudgeon are now quite easily obtainable.
SIZE GUIDE Gudgeon occasionally reach as long as 17 cm (7 in).

FISH TO AVOID

A number of other species found for sale in the UK from time to time are best avoided for a variety of reasons.

Roach (*Rutilus rutilus*) and bream
(*Abramis brama*)
Both will technically live in a small pond but are happiest in the wild in medium to large rivers or large still waters, and as they are mainly bottom feeders you will rarely see them. Bream in particular like to live in shoals and will churn up the bottom of a pond looking for food.
SIZE GUIDE Roach may reach 45 cm (18 in) and bream, which are also very deep-bodied, may grow to 75 cm (2½ ft).

Rainbow trout
Salmo gaideneri
These are quite commonly offered, especially the gold sports. This is a species of fast-flowing rivers, and although it may seem to do well in small fishery ponds in the UK many of those are spring-fed and up to 7 m (20 ft) deep. Few trout in these

ponds survive many weeks before being caught and removed anyway.
SIZE GUIDE Intensively reared rainbow trout can reach 1.2 m (4 ft) or more in only three years.

Barbel
Barbus barbus
Seen occasionally, this is first and foremost a species of very large fast-flowing rivers and is very unsuited to all but the largest pond. More significant, perhaps, is that these fish are very predatory and will eat surprisingly large prey, including your goldfish.
SIZE GUIDE The barbel can reach 90 cm (3 ft) in the wild.

Perch
Perca fluviatilis (Europe)
Perca flavescens (USA)
These are sometimes kept in cold water aquaria in a species tank and often do well. A good specimen of either species is very colourful, with a stunning spiked dorsal fin and gill rakers like razors. However, their beautiful camouflage coloration means that

they are very hard to see from the surface and they are so predatory that they will eat the majority of aquatic species smaller than themselves.
SIZE GUIDE *P. fluviatilis* is the larger species, reaching more than 45 cm (18 in).

Catfish
Ictalurus sp. or *Silurus glanis* (wels)
Catfish are sometimes recommended for ponds. In the UK their sale is under licence and you will rarely find them offered. They are not really suitable for ponds as they are capable of growing quickly and their huge mouths enable them to swallow quite large fish; smaller catfish have been known to settle for a bite out of an unswallowable fish, leaving it without a fin or tail. They feed mainly at night, making the other less nocturnal species an easy target. Consequently, they are not recommended for ponds unless kept on their own.
SIZE GUIDE Some members of the Ictalurid and closely related catfish families easily reach 50 cm (20 in), while the huge wels can grow to 3 m (10 ft) or even more in the wild.

Attacks by predators, where they do not end in the fish being eaten, can result in wounds and grazes. Fish in ponds can also be affected by other pests, some of them parasitic, which are treated as diseases.

PREDATORS
Dragonfly/damselfly larvae
The many beautiful, colourful and graceful species of damselflies and dragonflies are welcome at any pond as the adults hover and hawk, picking off nuisance insects (and beneficial ones too) in a ballet of aerial hunting skills. However, their larvae are a different proposition, creeping along the submerged stems of plants to pick off fry, small fish and tadpoles. You cannot avoid them, and many people consider the loss of a few fry a small price to pay for their appearance at their pond.

Great diving beetle
Dytiscus marginalis
A great all-rounder, the diving beetle can swim and fly. They are sometimes found near large sheets of glass, far from ponds, having mistaken the reflection from the glass as water and crashed into it. Both the adult, which can be well over 3 cm (1¼ in) long,

▼ Carnivorous great diving beetles can enter any pond

and the larvae will capture and eat fry and small fish.

Hydra
These remarkable freshwater invertebrates anchor themselves to an object in your pond and, using long stinging tentacles, capture both tiny organisms and creatures as large as fry or small fish.

POLLUTION
More than 90 per cent of major disease outbreaks are precipitated by water problems. This means, among other things, high levels of ammonia or nitrate; sudden changes in water quality (for example temperature, hardness or acidity); chemical pollution which may be wind-blown or from ground water run off; and lack of sufficient oxygen in the water.

When you encounter a disease problem, you must first take any obvious emergency action such as restarting a pump, unclogging a filter or removing dead or very sick fish. Before you medicate in any way, check the water quality of your pond. Poor water conditions stress your fish and suppress their immune system, which leaves them open to attack from disease and parasites, some of which are endemic (meaning your fish are already carrying the pathogen but have sufficient resistance to keep it at bay).

To limit the damage inspect your fish regularly and look for early warning signs – gasping at the surface, rubbing or scratching against the pond sides or base, failure to feed, clamped fins, general listlessness, any other unusual behaviour and all the visible signs of disease problems that follow.

PHYSICAL DAMAGE
Pond fish spawn are sometimes attacked by predators and may swim too fast in the confined space of your pond. This can lead to physical damage such as grazes, loose scales and open wounds. The fish will often recover of their own accord, but a very bad wound may need treatment by a vet. In most cases the fish is best treated individually by

▲ A dragonfly nymph eating a tadpole. The nymphs are also deadly predators of small fish

removal to a hospital tank or by immersion in the right anti-bacterial remedy, following the manufacturer's instructions. In the UK only vets can issue antibiotics and they will need to see the fish, regardless of the problem.

OXYGEN DEPLETION
Pond plants will produce oxygen through photosynthesis all day but not at night. A typical problem in a heavily stocked pond in warm weather and on still nights is oxygen depletion, as warm water contains far less oxygen than cold. Sadly the largest fish succumb first. Many pond owners now keep a large aquarium air pump or a dedicated pond air pump handy and use it throughout the summer. This is a good alternative to a fountain or waterfall, where the noise of night time use may irritate neighbours.

The air passing through the water adds only minimal oxygen. It is the disturbance at the surface of the water that helps gas exchange, with carbon dioxide escaping and oxygen entering.

PESTS AND DISEASES
Sores and ulcers
Not all apparent wounds are actually brought on by physical damage. Infection by *Aeromonas* bacteria can lead to horrible ulceration and koi and goldfish are especially badly affected.

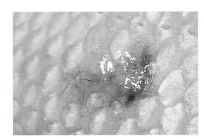

▲ **A bacterial ulcer on a goldfish**

It is now possible to prevent problems by using cultures of non-pathogenic bacteria to outcompete *Aeromonas* in the pond. However, a fish badly affected by ulcers may not be helped by this treatment retrospectively, and the use of external antibacterials as a bath or antibiotics if the bacteria are in the bloodstream may be the only way to cure it. If your fish are continuously subject to ulceration, consider the preventative use of competitive bacteria from spring onwards.

Over the last decade there have been reports of goldfish suffering from ulcers as the result of a debilitating viral infection that leaves them open to bacterial attack. Viruses cannot be successfully treated at the present time.

White marks

White marks are commonly seen on pond fish. Many of them are indicative of diseases and some are nothing to worry about, so it is

essential to be able to identify them and to know the possible causes.

Pinhead white spots

Spawning tubercles The males of many cold-water fish get small white spots – spawning tubercles – on their heads and gills when in season. These are a natural occurrence and not a sign of disease.

Whitespot A small parasite, *Ichthyophthirius*, is exceedingly common on all freshwater fish and appears as small white cysts on the body of the fish, the inhabitants feeding on its bodily fluids. They then leave the fish and form a tough pouch attached to a solid surface. Each pouch contains 1000 or more new parasites ready to burst out and attack another fish (or indeed the same one again). A few cysts will only irritate the fish but in large numbers they can eventually debilitate it, leaving it open to death from other causes.

Safe in its cyst the parasite is impossible to get at; all anti-whitespot remedies attack the free-swimming stage and therefore take a few days to work. You must treat the whole pond, but you can remove severely infested fish to a warmer hospital tank or vat – higher temperatures speed up the life cycle of the parasite, making it more quickly susceptible to treatment. Lacking a host the parasite dies within about a day, so a fishless pond will quickly be free of whitespot.

Viral growths

Cauliflower growths Fish with such growths are usually suffering from *Lymphocystis*, a harmless viral condition that comes and goes. Only if the lumps become damaged and infected is this likely to be a problem.
Waxy blobs White waxy blobs on members of the carp family are caused by another viral disease, carp pox. This is not fatal and is often treated like teenage acne – inevitable until the fish grows out of it. It is a typical problem in spring after a long cold winter.

Fish sometimes get skin tumours – both

◀ **Carp pox is rarely fatal**

benign and pathogenic – and they may appear similar to both these conditions.

White patches

Scale damage Any knock or graze may disturb body mucus or scales on the body of your fish and leave a paler patch. Unless pink patches of infection follow, these are nothing to worry about.
Sliminess of the skin White patches caused by extra heavy slime secretion may also appear over a wound, or as a result of water pollution or parasites on the fish's skin. You must try to isolate the cause and treat it.

▲ **Physical damage to this fish has led to fungal growths**

Fluffy white patches

Fungus (*Saprolegnia*) This will appear as brown, grey or white fluffy patches on the skin or fins. Invariably there will be a wound or scale damage underneath which has created dead material that the fungus is feeding on.
Mouth fungus/finrot These white-edged infections may look like fungus but are actually caused by bacteria such as *Aeromonas* or *Pseudomonas*. Again there is likely to be an underlying cause which needs investigation – often poor water conditions or the presence of another disease.

Other parasites

The **anchor worm** (*Lernaea*), **gill maggot** (*Ergasilus*) and **fish louse** (*Argulus*) are all crustacea and therefore distantly related to crabs and lobsters.

Female anchor worms fix themselves onto fish, appearing as a slim body with a

V-shaped tail – actually two egg sacs. They can be manually removed by clasping them close to the fish with tweezers and gently pulling, but the whole pond needs treating if they are present. Take advice on a suitable remedy – many of the treatments formerly recommended are now subject to bans, and can affect sensitive species such as orfe and rudd. Consider buying a topical remedy to treat the small wounds that are left after removal of the sacs.

The female gill maggot lives, as the name suggests, on the mouth and gills of fish. They are just a few millimetres long and it is the longer plump egg sacs of the females that gives them the 'maggot' part of their name. Badly affected fish have trouble breathing and may die. However, gill maggots are comparatively rare and unless you have recently added a fish to the pond (and even if you have), look for other causes of gasping fish, beginning with oxygen depletion, filter failure or pollution.

If gill maggots are the culprits, affected gills lose their healthy colour and look as if they have been sprinkled with pepper. As with other crustacean parasites, treat the whole pond, not the individual fish. There is also a fluke that attacks the gills of fish but it responds to similar treatments.

Argulus, the fish louse, is a flattened scale-shaped creature that can be hard to spot unless it is fastened to the soft underbelly of your fish. These lice clamp on and feed on the juices of your fish. As they may move from one fish to another they can transfer diseases.

Glochidia

Glochidia are the young larva of *Unio* and *Anodonta* mussels, which are sometimes sold as 'natural' filters. If you have bought them on that understanding you may wish to take them back to the shop and ask for a refund, for in fact they are no use whatsoever in filtration.

The glochidia are expelled from the gills of the mussels in the spring and embed themselves in the skin and gills of the fish for months. Tiny miniature mussels eventually fall off the bodies of the fish.

Leeches

Pisicola geometera is the best-known leech that affects pond fish, but there are many other species. Leeches are worm-like creatures which attach themselves to fish and feed off their blood. They are capable of transferring diseases, and while manual removal is effective when a fish has just one or two leeches feeding on it – for example after a winter spent lying deep and still in the pond – an infestation is a major problem that needs dealing with. A few leeches on a fish will do it little harm initially but large numbers are dangerous.

▲ Leeches are a rare problem but can be difficult to control

Because of their life-cycle, leeches are very difficult to eliminate from a pond. They produce tough leather-like cocoons around their eggs which resist chemical treatment. It is necessary to drain the pond completely, remove and destroy all the plants including the blanket weed on the sides, and leave the pond dry for up to a week.

Other problems

Dropsy is unmistakable – fluid builds up in the fish's body, the body swells and the scales lift up like a pinecone. Unfortunately it is also often untreatable and the causes are many and varied, including internal bacterial or viral infections, internal organ dysfunction, and problems arising from poor nutrition. Antibiotics are usually the only real hope,

▲ A one-eyed fish may continue to live for many years

often given by injection, as the fish is no longer feeding.

It may be possible to relieve the fish's symptoms a little by removing it to a hospital vat, slowly raising the temperature and adding salt to the water in order to help its osmotic balance.

Pop-eye is a condition where just the fish's eyes swell. It can be caused by physical damage and by infections and water pollution. A fish may lose just one eye and carry on regardless.

Cloudy eyes may be related to a parasite infection, physical damage, pollution or unrelated diseases. It is important to establish if the cloudiness is internal and therefore difficult to treat or is related to another disease problem and caused by the build-up of protective mucus on the body.

▲ Pop-eye has many causes, not all of which are fatal

9 • Maintenance

BARLEY STRAW

When added to pond water, barley straw produces an enzyme as it breaks down that appears to act as a natural algicide. It also encourages water fleas which feed on algae. Barley straw can be bought from specialist aquatic centres and should be added to the pond at the recommended quantities.

Above: Crystal-clear water can be expected in a well-planted, carefully stocked pond

A well-designed pond, if sited and planted correctly and not over-stocked, takes surprisingly little time to maintain. Within a couple of years of its creation the pond will establish its own natural balance and any maintenance should seek to retain this balance and maintain a high water quality. In order to minimize disruption, carrying out routine work little and often is by far the best approach. As with any aspect of gardening, pond maintenance varies over the seasons and carrying out the right task at the right time ensures success (see pages 138–9).

Maintaining water quality

Clear, healthy water relies on a complex ecological balance of water, gases, minerals, sunshine, plants and creatures. Despite good planning the balance may well be disrupted by environmental factors. Hot weather, bright conditions and high nutrient levels can cause algae to proliferate, smothering plants and shading too much surface area, thereby lowering oxygen levels and potentially killing the pond's inhabitants. This is usually only a problem early in the year when surface-shading plants and oxygenators (submerged plants) are not yet in full growth. If the algae does not clear of its own accord, it should be combated (see box) or, in the case of blanket weed, manually removed. Topping up the water level in summer with (mineral-rich) tap water will also disrupt the balance and encourage algae, so try to use collected rainwater wherever possible.

Unless you are keeping fish and fitting sophisticated filtration equipment, the best course is to adopt a natural means of controlling algae by using a range of plants to keep pace with its growth (see Functional plants, page 98).

Large fish can make pond water cloudy by disturbing the fine silt or clay on the bottom of the pond. The silt can be either manually removed or stabilized by covering with a layer of washed gravel.

In winter, water quality can suffer if ice covers the pond for a period of a few days, allowing toxic methane to build up with no means of escape. Create a hole in the ice by using a pond heater (you can plug it into the same electrical connection as the pump if that has been removed) or by placing a pan of hot water on the surface. Alternatively, when cold weather threatens, float a rubber ball in the pond and remove it from the ice each morning, leaving a hole. Remember to replace it again in the evening. Never break the ice with a hammer blow as this will traumatize and possibly kill fish and other pond life.

Maintaining the pond plants

Routine maintenance will help to keep your pond plants healthy, but because aquatic plants are generally more vigorous than conventional garden plants you need to be correspondingly more attentive. The regular removal of

dead and dying foliage is the most essential task as this prevents the build-up of decaying matter and the resultant loss of water quality.

Overcrowded plants are more prone to pests and diseases, especially in the summer, so regular division is important. Of course, encouraging wildlife to the pond will bring in beneficial predators and keep many of these pests at bay. Deadheading flowering plants will increase their flowering period, and in the case of certain potentially invasive plants will prevent their uncontrolled spread by self-seeding.

Submerged plants can be thinned at any time of year when they become too crowded. Do this little and often, avoiding too much disruption or algae may result. Floating plants can be raked to the side and removed as necessary. Larger floating plants can have their younger plantlets removed and refloated as required. Water lilies need to be divided when their flowering diminishes and their leaves become congested and are held vertically above the water. This is best done in summer every 3–4 years.

Below: Algae can proliferate in spring before floating-leaved and submerged plants begin to grow

Above: **The cotton wool-like masses of blanket weed can be periodically removed with a stout stick and left on the side of the pond overnight to allow creatures to crawl back into the water**

Above: **Vigorous oxygenating plants such as fish weed (*Largarosiphon major*) can be removed by combing the water with a rake.**

Above: **Duckweed (*Lemna* sp.) can quickly cover the surface of a pond and suffocate its inhabitants but is easily removed with a net or displaced with a fountain**

135

PLANT DIVISION

1 Lift the marginal plant (in this case the flag iris, *Iris pseudacorus*) and separate the fleshy rhizomes with your hands or a sharp knife.

2 Rinse the roots and trim them back to 5–10 cm (2–4 in). The leaves can also be trimmed back to limit water loss through the leaf.

3 The plant can then be replanted in the soil on the marginal shelf and weighted down with a stone.

Marginal plants can start to become overcrowded after three years or so, especially if they are contained in baskets. Division then becomes necessary. Many can be prised apart by hand, replanting the vigorous new growth portion of the divided plant and discarding the older. Tougher root systems can be cut with a knife or divided by placing two forks back-to-back and prising the root-ball apart. Spring is the best time to do this as cut surfaces heal more quickly, but be careful not to disturb breeding wildlife at this time of year. Do not divide plants during the dormant season (winter) as cold water can cause recently divided plants to rot.

Maintaining the structure

To keep the pond safe and looking good, edges and associated surfaces such as decks, bridges and stepping stones should be kept clean and well-maintained. In damp climates timber is especially prone to the build-up of slippery algae, but scrubbing away with a coarse brush is effective. Pond liners, especially the cheaper polythene and PVC types, can degrade and become brittle if they are exposed to sunlight for any length of time. Keeping the pond topped up will help to protect them.

Maintaining the equipment

Pumps in ponds 60 cm (2 ft) deep can be left in place over winter as the water is unlikely to freeze. However, in areas prone to severe winters pumps should be removed. If left in place they should be run once a week to keep them from seizing up. In fountain features with small reservoirs the pump should be removed and the water drained out of the reservoir. This is especially important

in the case of less frost-resistant terracotta or ceramic items where freezing water could expand and potentially shatter the feature. Clean pump filters as necessary to keep them from clogging up and losing performance.

Repairing the pond

A leaking pond will drain only as far as the level of the puncture and so can probably be repaired without draining out the whole pond and upsetting its balance. Cheaper polythene liners are rarely worth repairing as a split is generally an indication of deteriorating fabric, although patching kits for PVC and vinyl-based liners are available from aquatic centres. Rubber liners made from butyl are well worth repairing and patches can either be bought or made from liner offcuts. More serious tears to butyl liners are repairable by using a butyl welder to apply heat and pressure, but it is always preferable to call in a professional to do this.

Leaks in preformed fibreglass liners can be repaired with the fibreglass matting used for motorcar repairs or, in the case of small holes, a two-part resin compound. Try out the product on a non-essential area of the pond shell first. If the shell is cracked it may be due to subsidence in the soil beyond the liner. In this case it will need to be checked and the problem rectified before the crack is repaired.

Cracks in concrete ponds need to be repaired with mortar and sealed with a proprietary pond sealant. This is a more complex task and is best undertaken by a professional. Completely coating the pond with a flexible sealant is an option, but several coats are needed. An alternative is to line the whole pond with a flexible liner.

Emptying the pond

Emptying the pond is highly disruptive and should only be undertaken if the pond is leaking and the liner needs to be repaired, or when silt and debris in the pond bottom have accumulated to the point where the essential minimum depth has been lost. This might be every 4–5 years, although in smaller ponds it may be possible just to half empty the pond and remove a few bucketfuls of silt, thus minimizing the disturbance.

Summer is the best time to empty the pond as far as both wildlife and plants are concerned. The breeding season is over and hibernation has not yet started, and plants are able to re-establish themselves more quickly. Choose an overcast day to prevent the plants from wilting and have plenty of containers such as buckets and large plastic bins to hand in which to place the pond life. Fish need to be caught and transferred to a shaded holding tank filled with pond water. Spray a fine mist from a hose over the surface of the water every hour or so to keep up the oxygen levels. The water can then be siphoned or pumped out of the pond, but try to retain as much as possible as it contains the many micro-organisms so vital to the pond's healthy balance. If you have a waterfall or fountain, the submersible pump can be disconnected and attached to a hose for this purpose. Plants in baskets can be lifted as the water level drops and stored in shallow containers, but be careful not to damage the liner as you walk into the pond. Plants in soil on the marginal shelves can be left undisturbed.

Once the pond has been drained the silt on the bottom can be removed, using a plastic dustpan and brush (sharp metal tools could puncture the liner). The silt can be added to the compost heap, but keep some to reintroduce to the pond as it contains beneficial micro-organisms. Run the hose over the emptied pond, checking for any damage. Refill it as soon as possible, using as much of the original pond water as you can. If topping up with chlorinated or otherwise treated tap water, consider adding proprietary treatments to minimize the stress to fish. Restock the pond, checking plants and fish for signs of pests and disease and using the opportunity to divide and repot any plants.

Above: In autumn, stretch a net over the pond to catch falling leaves and consider installing a pond heater

Above: If the pond freezes over in winter, hold a pan of hot water on the surface to melt a hole in the ice

REPAIRING A BUTYL LINER

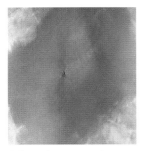

1 Once the puncture has been found the area around the hole is cleaned with water, followed by a solvent such as petrol, and left to dry.

2 Double-sided adhesive tape is applied to a piece of butyl. This patch is cut to a rounded shape to prevent any corners peeling back.

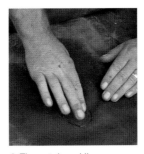

3 The patch and liner are then carefully heated (using a small blow torch or hot air gun) and the patch is stuck over the puncture.

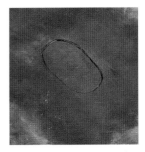

4 With the patch in place the pond can be refilled. To avoid stress to any fish in the pond use as much of the original pond water as you can.

Seasonal maintenance

SPRING

WATER AND PLANTS

- Check the water pH with a test kit and adjust if necessary
- Clear any early growth of algae and blanket weed
- Sink barley straw to inhibit algal growth and encourage water fleas
- Carry out replacement or additional planting
- Divide and transplant marginal and moisture-loving plants where necessary
- Reintroduce any frost-tender plants protected over winter
- Cut back old foliage left over winter to protect plants, taking care not to damage emerging young growth
- Mulch bog gardens and pond and stream margins to reduce weed growth and hold in moisture

FISH AND WILDLIFE

- Start feeding fish as the weather becomes warmer
- Protect frogspawn and tadpoles from fish and move to another pond if necessary

STRUCTURES AND EQUIPMENT

- Clean pond edgings and surrounding surfaces of potentially slippery algae and dirt
- Check pond edgings for looseness or frost damage and carry out any repairs
- Check bridges and decks for rot or corrosion and repair if necessary
- Check electrical equipment and cables for damage
- Service pumps and reinstall where removed over winter
- Lower pumps left in place to a position closer to the pond bottom
- Remove and store the pool heater if one has been used

SUMMER

WATER AND PLANTS

- Regularly check the water level and top up as necessary
- Check the water pH with a test kit and adjust if necessary
- In very hot, humid weather keep fountains and waterfalls running overnight to maintain oxygen levels
- Remove algae and blanket weed regularly if necessary
- Regularly remove dead and dying leaves on all pond plants
- Regularly deadhead flowering plants
- Check plants for signs of pests or disease and treat if necessary
- Collect seed for the propagation of aquatic plants
- Feed established plants with a slow-release fertilizer
- Divide and transplant established water lilies

FISH AND WILDLIFE

- Introduce new fish to the pond
- Feed fish with high-protein foods
- Check fish for signs of disease and treat as necessary
- Add protective nets or wires to deter pond predators (herons and pets) where necessary

STRUCTURES AND EQUIPMENT

- Clean biological filters to ensure the free flow of water
- Regularly clean fountain and waterfall pump strainers and filters to ensure efficient working
- Clean fountain jets and nozzles
- Keep water levels topped up in freestanding and wall-mounted fountain features to ensure that the pumps never run dry

AUTUMN

WATER AND PLANTS

- Remove dead and dying leaves from marginal plants and water lilies

- Cut back and remove excessive growth on submerged plants before natural dieback and subsequent decay occur

- Collect suitable material (young plantlets, winter buds) for propagation

- Remove any tender water plants to frost-free quarters

- Protect tender bog or moisture-loving plants with a thick mulch or by folding their decaying leaves onto the plant's crown

FISH AND WILDLIFE

- Feed fish on warm and bright days

- Provide artificial cover for fish to hide beneath over winter

- Provide a rock or log pile close to the pond for newts to hibernate under

- Leave some pond-side vegetation in place as cover for frogs and toads

- Allow some stems of marginal plants to remain standing for dragonfly larvae in the spring

- Leave some dead seed heads on plants for over-wintering invertebrates

STRUCTURES AND EQUIPMENT

- Place nets in position to catch autumn leaf fall and remove the leaves regularly

- Remove, clean and store pumps, filters and lights where not required over winter

- If pumps are left in place, raise them closer to the water surface to avoid mixing the cooler surface water with the warmer deep water

WINTER

WATER AND PLANTS

- Keep an area of water free from ice during extreme weather to avoid a build-up of toxic gases

- Brush snow from ice-covered ponds to allow light penetration and speed the melting of the ice

- Clear any remaining dead vegetation from the water before it decays

- Apply a mulch of compost or well-rotted manure to pond-side plants

FISH AND WILDLIFE

- Stop feeding fish as the water temperature drops

- Disrupt the pond as little as possible to avoid disturbing hibernating pond life

STRUCTURES AND EQUIPMENT

- Install a water heater to keep an area of ice-free water

- Float a flexible rubber ball on the water to absorb the pressure of expanding ice and remove daily to keep an ice-free area

- If the pond has frozen over, hold a pan of hot water on the surface to melt a hole in the ice

- Protect container water gardens or move them to a frost-free location

- Drain the water from less frost-resistant fountain pots and urns if damage is likely to occur

139

Conclusion

If your pond or water feature is well constructed, sensibly planted and correctly stocked it will be naturally healthy and easy to care for. Keep on top of your pond maintenance, working with nature and timing your tasks accordingly, and you will be rewarded with clear water, brimming with life, giving you endless pleasure for many years to come.

Resources

Bibliography

Archer-Wills, Anthony, *The Water Gardener*, Frances Lincoln, 1993
Baines, Chris, *How to Make a Wildlife Garden*, Elm Tree Books, 1985
Chinery, Michael, *The Living Garden*, Dorling Kindersley, 1986
Dawes, John, *The Pond Owners Handbook*, Ward Lock, 1998
Gibbons, Bob & Liz, *Creating a Wildlife Garden,* Hamlyn, 1988

Paul, Anthony & Rees, Yvonne, *The Water Garden*, Frances Lincoln, 1986
Robinson, Peter, *Water Gardening*, Dorling Kindersley, 1997
Seike, Kiyoshi, Kudo, Masanobu & Engel, David H., *A Japanese Touch for your Garden*, Kodansha Europe Ltd., 1980

Organizations and suppliers

Society of Garden Designers
The Institute of Horticulture
14/15 Belgrave Square
London SW1X 8PS
Tel 020 7838 9311
e-mail soc.gardendesign@btclick.com
www.society-of-garden-designers.co.uk

Royal Horticultural Society
80 Vincent Square
London SW1P 2PE
Tel 020 7834 4333
e-mail info@rhs.org.uk
www.rhs.org.uk

Association of Professional Landscapers
Horticulture House
19 High Street
Theale
Reading
Berks RG7 5AH
Tel 0118 9303132
e-mail hta@martex.co.uk
www.martex.co.uk/hta

British Association of Landscape
Industries (BALI)
Landscape House
Stoneleigh Park
Warwickshire CV8 2LG
Tel 024 7669 0333
e-mail info@bali.co.uk
www.bali.co.uk

HDRA
Henry Doubleday Research Association
Ryton Organic Gardens
Coventry CV8 3LG
Tel 024 7630 3517

e-mail enquiry@hdra.org.uk
www.hdra.org.uk

The Wildlife Trusts
The Kiln
Waterside, Mather Road
Newark NG24 1WT
Tel 01636 677711
e-mail wildlifersnc@cix.co.uk
www.wildlifetrust.org.uk

Equipment and liners
Blagdon Pump
Lambert Road
Armstrong
Washington
Tyne & Wear NE37 1QP
Tel 0191 417 7475
e-mail sales@blagdonpump.com
www.blagdonpump.com

Interpet
Vincent Lane
Dorking
Surrey RH4 3YX
Tel 01306 743747
e-mail interpet@interpet.co.uk
www.interpet.co.uk

Lighting for Gardens
1 Yew Tree Walk
Clifton
Beds SG17 5HN
Tel 01462 817000
e-mail sales@lightingforgardens.co.uk
www.lightingforgardens.co.uk

Lotus Water Garden Products
Junction Street

Burnley
Lancashire BB12 0NA
Tel 01282 420771

Oasis Water Garden Products
Oasis House
Deer Park Industrial Estate
Knowle Lane
Fairoak
Eastleigh SO50 7PZ
Tel 023 8060 2602
e-mail info@oasis-water-gardens.co.uk
www.oasis-water-gardens.co.uk

Plants and aquatic nurseries
Stapeley Water Gardens
London Road
Stapeley
Nantwich
Cheshire CW5 7LH
Tel 01270 623868
e-mail stapeleywg@btinternet.com
www.stapeleywatergardens.com

World of Water
Bicester Garden Centre
Oxford Road
Bicester OX6 8NY
Tel 01869 322489
www.worldofwater.co.uk
Contact for details of your local branch

Anthony Archer-Wills Ltd
New Barn Aquatic Nursery
Broadford Bridge Road
West Chiltington
West Sussex RH20 2LF
Tel 01798 813204

Picture acknowledgements

Key T = Top, TL = top left, TC= top centre, TR = top right; CL = centre left, C = centre, CR = centre right; B = bottom, BL = bottom left, BC = bottom centre, BR = bottom right

All illustrations by Debbie Roberts and Ian Smith, Acres Wild
All photographs by Ian Smith, except those listed below

Dave Bevan 1, 65, 66CR, BL, 67TL, 124TR, 125, 127, 128TC, BL, 129TR, BL, BR, 130, 131, 132CR, 133
Malcolm Birkitt 76BL (Designer: John Brookes)
Blagdon Pumps 90BL
Sally Court 72BR (Designer: Sally Court)
Garden Picture Library
   Marijke Heuff 42BR
   Michael Howes 137TR
   Jane Legate 137CR
   Michael Paul 60TR, 70C
   Howard Rice 61TC
   Gary Rogers 37

John Glover 5, 17TR (Holbeache Road, Shropshire), 35BR, 55 (Designer: Barbara Hunt)
Dr Bob Gibbons 24BR, 30BR, 78BC (Designer: Jean Goldberry), 81TR, 94TL (Designer: Sally Court; Sculptor: Lucy Smith)
Ian Pleeth 82BR, 86BC (Designer: Acres Wild)
Practical Fishkeeping, EMAP Active Ltd 122, 123, 124Bl, BR, 126, 128CR, 132TR, BR
Pedro Prá-Lopez 12TR, 19TL, 25T, 28TL, TR, 30TL, 58BL, 60BL, 77BR, 82BL, 85CR
John Raine, Lighting for Gardens 31B, 59BR, 91B
Debbie Roberts 9TR, 11TR, 42T
Tim Sandell 18B, 26B, 27BR, 54BL (Designer: Barbara Hunt)
Derek St Romaine 22BR (Designer: Cleve West), **Cleve West** 81C, 89TR

Gardens featured in the photographs by Ian Smith designed by:
Acres Wild 6, 7, 9TL, 14B, 20BR, 21TL, BR, 22BCL, 25BL, BC, 26TR, 28BR, 29TL, 32, 33TL, 34 (all), 35T, BL, 36TR, 40 (both), 44TR, 52TR, 56BL, 62/63C, 64TL, 68B, 73, 74, 75, 77CR, 78CR, 79TC, 80BL, BR, 81BL, BR, 82BR, 83T, 84, 85BL, 86B, 87TC, CL,

88TL, 89C, CR, B, 92, 93 (Ceramicist: Kate Mellors), 94TR, 95, 96, 103, 104BL, 105BR
James Aldridge 46, 47, Arcadia Garden Design 17B, 56TL, 64BL, 67B, 129T, 140, Julian and Isabel Bannerman 22BCL, James Basson 54TR, Christopher Bradley-Hole 8TL, 9TC, 15TR, 22TR, 50TR, 88CL, 104BR, Susanna Brown 69BR, David Brum 18TL, 52B, George Carter 14TL, Beth Chatto 16TL, 17TL, 21TR, 77TR, 97, 99, Terence Conran 50B, Julian Dowle Partnership 10TL, 88B, Guy Farthing 15BL, 71T, 80TR, Katerina Georgi 94B, Jacquie Gordon 80C, Kyoto Garden Association 16BR, 23TL, Arabella Lennox-Boyd 20BL, 79CB, Karen Maskell 69TC, Ryl Nowell 23TR, 50CR, Alan Sargent 72TR, Randle Siddeley 30TR, Conor Smith and Angie Reddy 134, Richard Sneesby 59TR, David Stevens 9B, 20TL, 23BL, 27TL, 28TR, 79CR, Tom Stuart-Smith 72TL, Julie Toll 44B, John Van Hage 38B, Mark Anthony Walker 8BR, 21BL, 25BR, 31T, 87TR, BL, Cleve West 15BR, 33BR, 135BR, Claire Whitehouse 71BL, Geoffrey Whiten 82T, Robin Templar Williams 19B, Pamela Woods 57TR, Patrick Wynniatt-Husey and Patrick Clarke 13BL, 22BCR, 76TR

Index

Page numbers in *italics* refer to photographs and illustrations. Plants and fish listed in chapters 7 and 8 are not included in this index.

Authors' acknowledgements

Firstly we would like to thank all of our clients, especially Judiey, Wendy, Jenny, Jean and Richard, Susan and Michael, Ann and Danny, Penny and Vas, and Margaret and Colin, for not only commissioning us to design their gardens in the first place but also allowing us back to take photographs.

We would also like to thank the contractors who install many of our designs and in particular, Landmark Design and Build Ltd (especially Mark,

Alan and Jim), M.W. Kelley Water Gardens, Alan Sargent Ltd, Farley Landscapes and The Outdoor Room Ltd and Dr Tim Acott Phd (pond digger).

Special thanks must go to all the other designers whose work features in the book and in particular, Cleve West, Barbara Hunt, Sally Court, James Aldridge and Emily Blake-Dyke for supplying images or allowing us to take photographs of the gardens they have designed. Thank you also to John Raine

for images of garden lighting, Emma at New Barn Aquatic Nurseries for allowing us to photograph the water lilies and last, but certainly not least, our fairy godmother, Carol Harwood.

Finally we are indebted to Cathy Gosling and Tess Szymanis at HarperCollins for putting their faith in us, our editor Diana Rayner for beating the text into submission and especially to Pedro and Frances Prá-Lopez at Kingfisher Design for making it all happen.